The Reluctant Migrant's Daughter

Li only realised who her parents were when she was five. The fifth of eight children to migrants from China, Li grew up in her family's shophouse in Kuala Lumpur, Malaya. Generally ignored by her elders, but regularly beaten and cursed by her guardian, Li still became infused with her father's longing to return to Shanghai, the home he left only reluctantly.

After a lonely childhood, Li had happy times at high school. She found the loving paternal figure she craved in the father of her future husband, only to lose him after a few years. Li's marriage was at times blighted by her relationship with her mother-in-law. Yet, Li remained loyal to her husband, raising four children while gaining university degrees in Singapore and Sydney.

Now in her early eighties, Li reflects on her life, from the early years of physical abuse and psychological deprivation, through the joys and trials of marriage, travel, racism, depression, and her hopes for her grandchildren's generation.

Li offers her story to give voice to events experienced by many but seldom discussed. She sounds a warning to immigrants who visualise a new, untroubled life, and suggests patience to host nations, where the traumas of new residents might not be known or understood.

Finally, Li's self-exploration enables her to recognise why she has always felt such a connection to China, a country she finally visited at the age of 45.

The Reluctant Migrant's Daughter

A memoir by Zhang Li

All rights reserved

Copyright © 2022 Zhang Li

Published by Zhang Jian Li

ISBN 978-0-646-86672-7

Dedication

> To the early migrants long gone,
> You carried your pain in silence.
> I salute you.
> May I give a voice
> To the sadness you carried
> And serve as a reminder of
> Your sad journey in life.
>
> Zhang Li

Contents

Forward 11
Zhang family tree 16
1 Historical context 17
    Shanghai 17
    Zhang family – the planning 18
    The best laid plans … 20
    Zhang family establishes itself in Nanyang 20
    A portrait of Zhang Yu – PaPa 23
    A portrait of Foong Ying – MahMah 25
    A portrait of Hilda 30
    A portrait of Little Miss Mary 35
2 The world of little Li 38
    Love in a traditional Chinese family 39
3 Japanese occupation of Kuala Lumpur 41
    Zhang family recovery 41
4 Back to the growing child 44
    The beginning, when I first recall 44
    Japanese marching song 44
    Chinese New Year's Eve 45
    Later during the Japanese occupation 48
5 New domestic arrangements 49
    Ah Chieh, the young wife 49
    A portrait of Grandma See and foot binding 55
    Domestic politics in the Zhang household 57
6 More Zhang family memories 61
    Zhang Yu, Ah Chieh and little Li 61

    Yam cakes and a fall down the stairs 62

    A rickshaw ride 63

    The china doll 64

    Caning 66

    Opium dreams 71

7 "I love school" 75

8 Reinstatement of British rule 77

    More young migrant workers 77

    The Zhang family business 81

    The radio 85

9 My siblings 87

    Brother Kwok - shattered dreams? 87

    Sister Meng 90

    My second brother, Yeh 93

10 Life after Zhang Yu, 1950 - 1952 97

11 Teenage Life 100

    The world of boys, 1954-1957 100

    The happy student years, 1958-1959 107

    Portrait of KM, my father-in-law 111

    Grace, my mother-in-law 116

    Sister-in-law Chun 120

12 Marriage 123

    The 1960s 123

    The last word about Grace 127

13 Australia the first time around 136

    Melbourne, 1967 136

    A musical interlude 138

An episode of a cat that loved curries	138
Back to studying	140
Last months in Melbourne, 1969	144
14 Politics in Malaysia, 13 May 1969	**147**
Death was just around the corner	148
Aftermath of 13 May 1969	152
15 Reluctant migration	**156**
Time to say "Goodbye Malaysia"	156
Sydney, 1977-1979	162
Melbourne, 1990	168
Becoming Australian	169
16 The growing years	**172**
Back to the family	172
17 A portrait of conflict – love and hate	**174**
18 My Chinese Odyssey	**180**
Life as a mature-age student	180
Xi'an	182
Yan'an	188
Xi'an again	190
Shanghai	193
A Portrait of Luk May	198
More Shanghai	200
Beijing	200
19 More travel	**203**
Back to Sydney, 1986	203
The skiing years, 1987 - 1988	204
Skiing, fun and games	205

20 The good years 210
  Harbin, 1993 217
  India, Nepal and Thailand 220
21 My cup runneth over, 1999 - 2000 224
22 Other endings 229
23 Have I come full circle? 230
  Music in the night 230
  A final word 232
Epilogue 235
Acknowledgements 238
Photograph credits 239

Forward

The Reluctant Migrant's Daughter starts with an account of my family's migration from Shanghai to Malaya. In 1932 my father Jen, a 19 year old, and my mother Luk May, aged 16, were instructed by Jen's father to join the family business in Kuala Lumpur, British Malaya. He was a reluctant migrant, but filial piety dictated that he did as he was told. In 1977 his daughter Li found herself a reluctant migrant as she and her family of six left Malaysia for Australia. They left for the beliefs held by both Li and her husband Kit.

This account is also autobiographical, a human story, the emotions of a growing child's journey. One finally told from my perspective, experiences that even my own siblings, let alone my husband or children, only partially know or understand.

The first part of Li's life revolves around migrants. All her adult relatives were migrants. She, of all her Malayan-born siblings, seemed to have absorbed a love for a place and a country she did not know: Shanghai, China. It was from Zhang Yu, the family's pioneer and leader, his younger wife Ah Chieh, his senior wife and Li's guardian MahMah, and her parents that Li picked up those sentiments and learnt about life. The curious child listened to the conversations of the adults, conversations she recalls, even in her old age.

It was a harsh upbringing, yet rich in feelings. Li learned intense emotions: longing, fear, sadness and the pain of rejection. She also learnt to love, and love made her vulnerable. She held no hatred in her. It seemed a long childhood. It was an entire lifetime for Li.

Perhaps Li's major mistake was to adopt her opium-addicted guardian as her role model – although, in fairness, MahMah was the only adult around after gentle Ah Chieh left. But the fact remains that MahMah was an independent woman, while other Chinese women were submissive and docile. The clever ones had to be manipulative to get their way. Not MahMah!

Western education and ideas also had their influence on the growing Li. The lonely and neglected childhood also gave her plenty of time to think and develop as she wandered around. This all made Li independent. She wanted to be her own person, not somebody's lackey.

In looking up to MahMah, Li failed to learn the social niceties of life. Husband Kit asked what harm there was in smiling, even at someone she didn't like? But MahMah had been the lady boss. She seldom smiled and never needed to be nice to anyone. Li failed to realise that pretence is part of life. People are complex, they play games. Mother-in-law Grace saw Li's weakness. She said Li could not win if she chose to fight instead of obeying her. Grace had a smile for everyone and could be most charming.

In her old age, Li learnt that people have different beliefs, different priorities in life. That people are basically self-centred. But who are we to judge?

I hope my book gives hope to others. To those who feel untalented and have been told they are of little worth. I have been through that. Yet I cannot complain about this life, for I have had many rewards. I have found much beauty in nature and in humankind. Besides sadness and pain I have known joy and happiness. In my old age I do not want hatred or grudges. I wish to lie down each night untroubled, to think of the past with a smile on my lips and sleep in peace. That I am able to sleep in peace I am thankful for.

There are many roles we have to play in this life. For me it has been daughter, wife, mother, friend. It is too difficult to play each one equally well. I put too much into being the good wife and not enough into the patient mother. I spent most of my life sublimating my thoughts, desires and career prospects to support my husband. My learned feelings of inadequacy made me believe that I should do that, especially when faced with the certainty exhibited by others. I made myself sick because of it, diagnosed in my 30s with acid damage to the lining of my stomach. I have been taking medication for that ever since.

Now I am free of that past. I have paid my dues. I earned what I have and enjoyed, even though I rarely received the credit for my efforts. Now I feel the need to explain the person I am and how I got here. Perhaps it will make sense of the impatience and quickness to take offence that I have displayed at times. I find that there is no need to fabricate situations, like in a novel, as I only need to relate my history as it happened.

For the younger generations I wish a better understanding than I had of life and its complexities. For me, my salvation is the willingness to love. Love has eased my journey through life.

Looking back, I find it a strange phenomenon that the little child Li could absorb from the adults in her family a love for a place she had not seen or known, for Shanghai. Yet I know it happens because it happened to me. And now I find my pride in being Chinese, particularly in being Shanghainese, long suppressed since moving away from my Zhang family, has resurfaced. Shanghai does not have the reputation for ancient scholarship and tradition held by other major centres in China, but it has dynamism and entrepreneurialism at its core. Like my Zhang family.

My early years also ignited a love of history. My sad childhood gave me an affection for literature. My yearning and longing for love gave me an affinity with the English poets who seemed to be searching for perfection in an imperfect world. I learned to appreciate poetry, nature and tranquillity.

My final message is to migrants.

After he had been ill for some years, I took my husband, Kit, for a final trip to Malaysia, hoping it would give him some joy. I thought the memories of a happy childhood and youth would do him good. The truth was, after the initial fortnight he wanted to go home. Home was Australia, where he had lived for 43 years. He loved this country, his country. In his last years Kit's favourite walk was along the pier opposite the casino at Pyrmont. You can see Sydney Tower and other large buildings in the city from there. Further down the walkway is a view of the Sydney Harbour Bridge. It was from his wheelchair that he silently absorbed these scenes. Each week for four years this was what he enjoyed.

For me, Sydney has been home for 45 years. Can I tell migrants to Australia and their children that it is not wrong for the elders with heavy emotional baggage to have affection for the country of their birth and upbringing. Where there is love there can be no wrong. Neither is it wrong for Li to have affection for her parents' homeland.

My favourite walk is along the foreshore outside the back gate of the block of apartments where I live. This soothing scene of much beauty has a golf course on my left, while on my right I look across the waters to Exile Bay. I have lived in this area since 1999, and in Sydney since 1977. I feel love and gratitude. This is HOME.

Zhang family

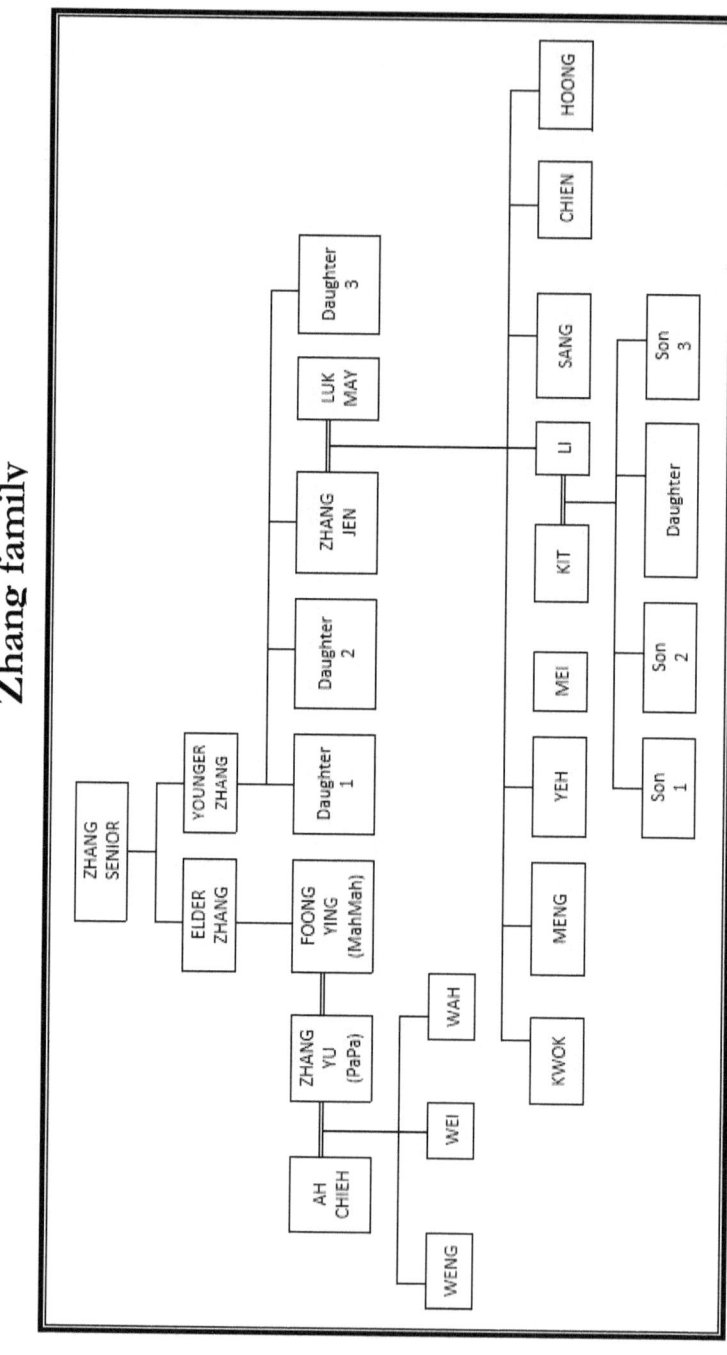

1 Historical context

Shanghai

At the turn of the 20th century westerners are very active in Shanghai. The western powers have forced their way to the East, led by the British. In 1918 there are 19 treaty powers in Shanghai. Foreigners wield more power in the Shanghai international settlement than the Chinese, even though it is on Chinese soil.

With its port, Shanghai is the busiest city in China, while Beijing is the intellectual capital and centre of student protests. The British and French are powerful and they live well in Shanghai. There are other European powers, including the Germans and Italians. Even the Belgians and Austrians are there. The number of Russians increases after 1917 as intellectuals flee across the border, preferring to find a new home rather than stay on Russian soil amidst the turmoil that is the aftermath of the revolutions. The French are unhappy that the Russians have taken on lowly paid jobs, for they are still "white men". Young Russian girls are rumoured to be available at a price in Shanghai.

The presence of the Japanese, the latest power group in Shanghai, has been increasingly felt since the end of the 19th century. Shanghai has so many foreigners it receives a new nickname: Bastard child of China.

Zhang Yu grows up in Shanghai. He sees the arrogant foreigners moving around, but meticulously avoids them. The locals have been warned not to run afoul of them, particularly the Japanese. Yet years later, in 1942, he meets them in Malaya, almost to die at their hands!

Zhang Yu has his dreams. For him, Shanghai is the Paris of the East. He will bring the world of fashion from Shanghai to Nanyang, the lands of the south, where he will make his fortune.

Zhang family – the planning

It is winter, January 1929. Four men in long Chinese gowns are huddled over a wooden table in a full-brick house that implies some wealth. It is around 20 kilometres from the Shanghai town centre, a good distance from the rowdy politics of the city. They have just finished their final meeting, making plans to scope out a business venture in Kuala Lumpur, British Malaya, for the benefit of the family.

Shanghai winters are always cold, bitterly cold, so there is a charcoal burner in the room. The men all share the family name Zhang: two brothers over the age of 40, a distant relative, and Zhang Yu, who is 27.

The Zhang brothers are very close. The elder brother has been more successful and will put more funds into the new business venture. It is unfortunate that he has only one child, a spoiled daughter named Foong Ying. Elder Zhang is glad that she has married the capable and reliable Zhang Yu. Elder Zhang will make the first trip to Kuala Lumpur with son-in-law Yu. Also going is Elder Zhang's distant nephew, the money manager. He can do the sums, and is vital for the new investment. He later returns to live in Shanghai, as that is his preference.

Although the younger Zhang brother, owner of this house, elects to stay in Shanghai, he reassures Elder Zhang that his son, Jen, would follow in a few years. It is a great relief to Elder Zhang, for there is family back up. Young Jen will be groomed for his future role in Malaya.

Meanwhile, as the four men meet inside the house, Jen sits in the backyard playing with his younger sister. Jen is a strapping boy of 15. He has his father's dark eyes, thick eyebrows and thin high nose. Jen's father knows that Jen is neither brilliant nor a born leader, but a very good follower. Besides, he is a dutiful son. They have already started looking for a wife for him.

Zhang Jen's parents and Li's grandparents

Jen is happiest eating watermelon. Last summer he consumed a whole melon all by himself in one sitting.

Jen will learn from and be guided by Yu, who is the leader and has the brains. The family in Shanghai will have a good income from dressmaking and dry cleaning businesses in Nanyang. Jen's two married sisters will also benefit. Indeed, a few years later, the younger sister marries and also migrates, settling in Ipoh. She never experienced the life-long yearning to return to Shanghai that Jen, my father, had.

The team of three manage a successful trip in 1929. Yu remains in Malaya for a few extra months; he has to sort out the red tape with the British Administration. In addition, the time-honoured practice of bribery – kopio money – has to be observed with the locals. The amounts are not large, but the middlemen and clerks, Eurasians and Indians, must be paid.

For some reason, the originally selected two shops cannot be obtained and two other shops further up the street are acquired instead. However, everything is in place for the two businesses by early 1932. The planning was almost perfect, but life is unpredictable ...

The best laid plans ...

In the 1930s British Malaya is thriving. It is a beautiful, promising country with gentle people who appear content with living along the rivers nestled in the bosom of mother nature. Exploitation of natural resources is bringing changes. Chinese investors began tin mining in Perak and Selangor in the 1820s. In 1872 it was recorded that there were 40,000 Cantonese and Hakka miners there from southern China. By 1931 the number had risen to 110,000 miners of Chinese origin.

The other big product was rubber. The British started the plantations and brought the labour from India. The demand for car tyres led to a boom in Kuala Lumpur, both in population and business. By 1930 Malaya was known as the world's largest natural rubber producer. Malayan rubber and tin brought immense wealth to the British.

For the Zhang family, coming to Malaya is a combination of foresight and luck. The family fortune starts to rise. Yu indeed has business acumen, but the family's flaw is that they want to keep their earnings liquid, in gold bars, instead of investing in their new country. Had they done so, they would likely have become one of the richest families in Kuala Lumpur, but the Zhangs' plan is to take their wealth home to Shanghai and buy property there. They failed to recognise the growth of the Chinese Communist Party, born in Shanghai, or foresee the Revolution in 1949.

Their other weakness is that everything depends on one man: Zhang Yu. It never enters the minds of the Zhang brothers that Yu could be dead well before either of them.

Still, there is a story to tell, a wealth, not of gold bars, but of human emotion ...

Zhang family establishes itself in Nanyang

In 1932 the Zhang family is acclimatising to its new country. Zhang Yu and his wife, Foong Ying, are reaching

30 years of age. Yu's support team includes a number of relatives. Foong Ying's 19 year old cousin Jen – my father, the reluctant migrant – and his newly married 16 year old bride, Luk May, are among them, as planned back in January 1929.

As the oldest members of the family in Malaya, Yu and Foong Ying are the Patriarch and Matriarch. The children of Jen and Luk May will call them PaPa and MahMah, while calling their own parents Ah Sook (uncle) and Ah Sum (aunt).

Several dressmakers, all of whom had been apprenticed to a shifu (master) in Shanghai, are brought over to make western clothes, women's evening clothes in particular, as well as an expert in Chinese cheongsams. The dry cleaning experts also come, one of whom is Ha See Fu, a bachelor and a very good worker in his twenties with experience in ironing western suits. He remained until the business closed down, and died a few years after it did.

The planning is good. Merchandise is sourced from Shanghai, along with more young workers as required. The kitchen has two full-time cooks to feed them a diet of mostly bean curd dishes and peanuts, ingredients from home. Canvas bunks are situated on the first floor of the shop, next to the work area. It is expected that in a few years the young men will be sent back to Shanghai to get married and bring their brides back to Kuala Lumpur. As business prospers, Yu plans to help his workers buy modest homes. Whether they eventually return to Shanghai or retire in the new country will be up to them.

*

It is 1933 and the two new shops stand out in Batu Road, a part of town reasonably busy with the British and Europeans. In the first shop, the Shanghai Dressmaking Co, a dummy wearing a Western-style white wedding dress poses behind the glass of the window on the left. In the other window is a Western-style red evening dress and matching red high heel shoes. By the shoes are boxes of silk flowers, intended for brides or any other fancy occasion.

The two Zhang family shophouses as they look in 2022

In the shop are glass cases filled with beaded evening bags, porcelain and ceramic vases, and boxed sets of pillowcases and bedsheets for sale. Then there are the rolls of silks, brocades and taffeta. Expensive magazines displaying the latest fashions litter small side tables that sit adjacent to a large fitting room with thick curtains. Beyond that is a room filled with workers and eight treadle Singer sewing machines, the first in Malaya. Almost everything is brought from Shanghai, including the excitement.

Oriental International and Cleaning (OIC) is a much simpler shop. A light brown suit is displayed in one window and a white sharkskin suit in the other, the latter being all the rage. They are available for bridegrooms and best men to rent from the dressmaking shop. Afterwards, they are cleaned at OIC and returned to the dressmaking shop to rent out again. A long polished counter waits for customers to rest their clothes on as they request dry cleaning. Two receptionists check the clothes and issue receipts. The maximum wait time is three working days, normally two. Carpets are left on the floor until the young workers carry them through to the back for cleaning.

This is a good year. The shops thrive and a birth takes place in the Zhang family. The first baby of Jen and Luk May is greeted with much excitement. The boy's name, Kwok, means healthy country. The boy indeed grows healthy and happy, doted on by MahMah. She has less time to fight with her husband now she has a child to play with.

Come 1935 and Luk May is pregnant again. In August, she has a daughter. Not as good as another male, the Zhangs feel, but acceptable. This child is named Meng, and she seldom gives anyone any problem. The servants look after Kwok and Meng. They are followed by another son, Yeh, and daughter, Mei, at which point MahMah starts losing interest, even though she is glad there are many offspring. After all, these are the children of Jen, her cousin, whom she calls brother. They, and the children born later, all share an unusual familial shape around the elbow joint.

A portrait of Zhang Yu – PaPa

I was only nine when Zhang Yu, my most senior uncle whom I called PaPa, passed away. Thanks to a vivid memory, I recall many instances with him as if I am watching myself, little Li, in a movie.

In my earliest recollection of him, little Li is a child of five. She is seated at the table with PaPa for breakfast. Everyone else is asleep, but Li is usually up and wandering around before the rest of the family. The kitchen staff are always active early, meaning there is a guaranteed supply of plain congee with small dishes of peanuts, radishes, pickles, bamboo shoots and canned fish. Sometimes there are large pieces of salted pork. PaPa often has bread and butter, of which he is fond.

It is a time of benevolent tolerance towards children, although most adults have little time to play with them. PaPa is always busy, but I don't recall a single harsh word or punishment from him to me or my siblings. Discipline was left to his wife, MahMah. I'm not sure he knew about the harsh beatings, although no one could miss her cursing. Perhaps he had grown immune to it.

Breakfast is always a fun show for little Li. She watches in fascination when PaPa eats congee and the fried peanuts disappear into his mouth. As one peanut goes in, the skin of a chewed peanut comes out. How does he do it so fast?

On toast days there is even more entertainment. PaPa spreads thick canned butter onto the bread. Then the whole thing is in his mouth, butter oozing through the gaps between his front teeth. The wiggly yellow worms in his mouth make Li clap with glee. PaPa is unperturbed by her reactions. He finishes his breakfast, straightens his shirt, then heads downstairs to do the books before opening the shop.

Not infrequently after this ritual, a soft thud will sound: Li's head slipping onto the breakfast table, deep in sleep again.

*

PaPa had a stern look about him, but he was known to be kind and charitable. His complexion was dark for a Chinese person. He was of average height, broad-shouldered with small eyes, not talkative, but he spoke when necessary.

He was often called upon when there were problems within the Malayan Shanghainese community, and was president of the Shanghainese Association until he died. The receipts for his donations were kept under the glass top of his office desk. It was all there for years after his death.

Under him, the business flourished. Had PaPa lived it would have continued to grow, but he died aged 47. It was 1949 and Malaysia was recovering well from WWII. I am confident he would have married me and all my sisters to Shanghainese businessmen and bankers. Our lives would have been different had he been in them for longer.

A portrait of Foong Ying – MahMah

Foong Ying – MahMah to me and my family – was only a little lady, around four foot ten and slight of build. She had small, single-lidded eyes and often squinted. Her thin lips could curl into a cruel sneer or a cold crooked smile. A small nose and a small face. Everything about her was small. I have seen photos of MahMah with her friend Hilda. She was well dressed, with a China doll fringe, standing in front of Hilda's Rolls Royce and smiling into the camera. I thought she looked very stylish and cute.

MahMah damaged me. She caused me so much physical and mental pain during my childhood, but I never hated her. Her swearing was second to none and familiar to all who knew her. Her nastiness was the same, whether it was to the errant worker or to "brother" Jen's children. There was no pretence in her. She never manipulated or played the games that other women did. I admired her for her decisiveness, firmness and the courage to follow through on what she believed in. However, she lacked the experience and imagination required to run the business her husband's sudden death left behind. He left without warning, and she was thrust into managing what he had handled alone. Jen had shown no promise, but MahMah loved power and was unlikely to give it up. In any case, Jen was not strong and had no ambition. The reluctant migrant was still a follower, not a leader.

Yu's death left a vacuum. No one could control MahMah. She trusted no one, sought no advice from anyone. She did not tolerate fools. Ah Chieh thought that the opium was to blame, but I think she was already flawed. The opium just did the rest.

I was the only one who listened to her childhood stories, although I was a child myself.

MahMah had been an only child, doted upon. She was taken to school, piggybacked by a servant, and seldom did her own walking. She was intelligent and often topped the class. She was good at recitation and did not need to put in too much study to master the poems and passages from the classics. She was the apple of her father's eye.

Yu was from a poor background, but had proved himself as the best worker at the Shanghai shop owned by MahMah's father, and won over the boss's daughter. Winning her was easier than living with her, for she was petulant and wilful. She had the habit of reminding him that she was the rich man's daughter.

However, through the 1930s, MahMah was a good supportive wife as the two shops became established. Then came a third shop selling leather goods, managed by a trusted fellow Shanghainese until business was briefly disrupted by the Japanese Occupation.

It was heartbreak and hard work in 1941 when the dressmaking and dry cleaning shops were looted. News came that the leather goods shop had also been totally looted. The manager begged Yu to let him have the now empty shop to run a small business so he could feed his growing family. Yu agreed. Lo and behold, before long the shop was open, offering for sale an ample range of leather goods. The clever manager had been able to hide the goods and now they were worth a tidy sum! Each time the manager's name was mentioned MahMah would spit. The Shanghainese community knew of the deceit, but he was now an established businessman.

The Japanese occupiers encouraged small businesses, and soon the Shanghai Dressmaking Co was doing well again. Affluent Chinese became customers. One wealthy lady who turned up often was Hilda. Hilda would arrive in her chauffeured Rolls Royce to pick up MahMah for lunch. MahMah was also her regular Mah-jong companion. They were introduced to opium together. Rich ladies with plenty of time on their hands found new hobbies and new thrills!

By this time MahMah was in her late thirties. As early as 1933 she had suspected that she was infertile and started toying with the idea of a concubine for PaPa. In 1943, Ah Chieh joined the Zhang household, bringing her mother and younger sisters.

MahMah organised a Chinese marriage for PaPa and Ah Chieh. Polygamy was not uncommon in Malaya in those days. MahMah declared to all and sundry that she was not the jealous type and that her husband deserved to have children, which a young wife could provide. She did get jealous. Ah Chieh was not only young but beautiful, and Yu fell in love with her. However, Ah Chieh accepted her place in the pecking order. She was always respectful, submissive and never provocative. Fifty years later Ah Chieh told me that life had been a balancing act. Yu had to get permission to visit her in her bedroom. Each time he would return to an angry female who would pummel him!

When Ah Chieh had her first child, a boy, MahMah was beside herself with excitement. She absolutely doted on this child, who showed such a strong resemblance to her husband. Ah Heng, the baby amah, claimed his head and neck were miniatures of Zhang Yu. MahMah always showed a cold exterior, but it cannot be denied that she loved her husband. They did have their happy times in China, and even in Malaya.

According to my sister Meng, Ah Chieh's entry into our lives marked the beginning of our neglect. The servants had new instructions. Ah Chieh and her children were to receive attention before Luk May and her children. The instructions came from MahMah.

*

When my mother-in-law, Grace, told me in 1958 to take herself for my role model it was too late. Kit told me that his mother was one of the best drivers around, but I knew she was indecisive and took ages to cross the road. I could not understand his adoration of someone who admitted to being a timid driver, who took over an hour to decide what to wear and repeatedly told me how beautiful she was! So much of me was already made and Grace was completely new to my world. The warning signs about Grace's hold over Kit were all there, but I was too naïve and chose to ignore them at my own peril.

Yet I had little choice: MahMah was already my role model. She was decisive and authoritative, and I admired that. It was from MahMah that I learnt to brush my teeth. I watched her go, left right, left right, ending with the retching sounds caused by the tongue cleaner. I had no tongue cleaner, but as a child I ended my brushing routine with the same spluttering sounds.

During her opium smoking sessions at home I was the only child hovering around. I studied her closely. In my opium games with other children I faithfully reproduced the puffing noise from the pipe, but more so her face: the expression of pleasure that spread across her features, the roll of her eyes to the ceiling and the sigh of bliss that escaped her lips!

*

I do not know what made MahMah so hard and cruel. I know so little of her past. I never heard her mention her mother. Did something happen in her childhood?

I was terrified of MahMah. My fear made me run into instead of past her on more than one occasion. Her fights with PaPa terrified all the Zhang children. She would throw things, anything small and close at hand, cups, plates, vases, shoes, and once a small electric fan. The only person who could control her was PaPa, but she could infuriate him. She once got him so mad that he overturned the large sitting room table made of heavy wood. It took three people to put it upright again.

After PaPa passed away, badly behaved young workers were sent to MahMah for disciplining. I remember one occasion when a local Chinese youth received a session from her. He was new and had only one eye. In our sitting room upstairs MahMah ripped into him, telling him that he lost his eye because he and his parents had done evil things. She swore at him, and I winced at her cruel words. I felt distressed when I saw tears seeping from his good eye. But as I grew older I feared her less. She also became more humane.

*

Grace told me I should hate MahMah. No, I never hated her. She was predictable. I could cope with people who were predictable. I feared those who played tricks on me. I remember occasions when MahMah was kind to me. Once I was very sick when I was about 12. She made an effort and took me to a western doctor. I was given antibiotics and recovered after four days. Twice she bought me a little gold bracelet. She was at my father-in-law's wake and gave a handsome fifty dollars to the bereaved family. But most of all, I was grateful that she had not given me away in marriage to a middle-aged Shanghainese businessman when I was twelve. Ah Chieh told me this fellow had been attracted by my bright eyes. MahMah's reply was "No way, old fart, I am not giving you this young thing." My father would never have objected, MahMah would have received a big ang pau and they would have one mouth less to feed. Lucky for me she did not like that guy!

MahMah's gambling was also second to none, taking part in the local gambling syndicates. The biggest was the Empat Ekor, a numbers game, another was Chee Fah. I remember that the adults could convert their dreams into numbers, especially if their dreams had animals. MahMah also tossed for lucky numbers before the altars of the gods; goddess Kwan Yin was a favourite. Later, horse racing was her choice, thanks to Hilda. Lottery tickets littered the house. Cash was taken from the till at the dry cleaning shop and an entry left there as an expense item. No one dared query her. These things did not happen when Yu was alive.

MahMah also had a weakness for the opera. Ah Heng, the baby amah, was absolutely delighted when Hilda introduced MahMah to the Cantonese Opera. Ah Heng was the closest to MahMah after Yu went. She used baby Weng to manipulate MahMah. Ah Heng, the lonely spinster, although no great scholar, could read and write simple Chinese. She read about heroes in the warring kingdoms of China's past and loved watching portrayals of them by the young Hong Kong actors. Ah Heng encouraged MahMah to sponsor and adopt them as godsons. It was an expensive hobby. Entertaining and feeding the actors had been costly for Hilda in Hong Kong; so too for MahMah in Kuala Lumpur. The Zhang children would have to feed on simpler food and make do with less. Hilda, however, was more extravagant than anyone else.

A portrait of Hilda

Hilda was the favourite visitor of the Zhang children, and influenced our lives in more ways than one, directly and indirectly. She was a most unusual individual, showing interest in children at a time when few thought much about them.

It was 1933 when fashionable Hilda from Hong Kong turned up at the Shanghai Dressmaking Co. Hilda's father was a rich businessman who died young, leaving his only child a row of shops in central Hong Kong. Hilda sold the shops one by one, going through a fortune with great ease. She visited Singapore and Kuala Lumpur every year, one classy lady who was always looking for excitement.

As did all the rich in Kuala Lumpur, Hilda found her way to the top dressmakers. She received special attention from Yu. Hilda wanted the best looking clothes and money was no problem. Before long Hilda struck up a great friendship with the owner's wife. She also met my father, Jen. Hilda's mother took a liking to this good looking young fellow from Shanghai and decided to adopt him as a godson, as she had no sons. Hilda was thus a godsister to Jen. Hilda assessed Jen and decided that he was no Zhang Yu. She even gave him a fond nickname, something like Dum Dum!

In their search for excitement it was Hilda who encouraged MahMah to smoke opium. Of the two expensive opium pipes MahMah used, one was presented by Hilda's husband. The centre piece of the pipe, the teak bulb, sits in my glass cupboard at this very moment!

Two women smoking opium

Hilda had met a scion from one of the newly rich families in Kuala Lumpur. The two rich spoilt young people fell in love and married in haste, a tempestuous relationship that was never going to last, because neither knew how to compromise.

Hilda's marriage broke down. She loved people, and had foolishly acquired a protégée, an attractive young lady she rescued from homelessness in Hong Kong. Her husband had fallen for the protégée. It was indeed a cruel blow!

Hilda, in her spendthrift style, employed the most talented and, of course, most expensive solicitor in Kuala Lumpur. Having suffered physically and emotionally, she was not going to give in without a fight. Her husband was, of course, no pushover and he also employed a top solicitor. It was financially draining. When Mr R, Hilda's solicitor, learnt of her connection with Zhang Yu's wife, he started to send his clothes for dry cleaning. It lasted for the duration of the court case and beyond, never paying a cent! I remember Mr R's driver picking up the clothes.

The bitter divorce proceedings took many years. Hilda was granted the marital home, a beautiful house in an exclusive hill district. The bitterness manifested itself in a partially wrecked house. Hilda's husband trashed the place. I saw the broken statues in the garden, the broken tiles and bathtubs, while the sitting room and the stairs were strewn with broken glass. It was certainly not a sight for a ten year old child, but Hilda's errand girl, Miss Mary, had gone to check on something and taken me along. Little Li was always available to go out!

After the bitter divorce Hilda returned to Hong Kong. Her house was sold cheaply because of the bad damage. Years later we met the new owner of Hilda's house, a suitor of my sister Meng's classmate. He told us that the task of clearing the debris was long and tedious.

Life is strange: it was in Hong Kong that my future mother-in-law met Hilda. Grace was taken to Hilda's mansion for one of her big lunch gatherings and was a witness to Hilda's generosity. She saw Hilda give away some coats to those who dared ask. It was so like Hilda. She was generous to a fault.

In Hong Kong, for diversion and excitement, Hilda started to mix with actors from the Cantonese Opera world. It was expensive. She was to introduce these people to MahMah. The Hong Kong opera stars frequently toured and performed in Kuala Lumpur. After Zhang Yu's death, Hilda would phone from Hong Kong, asking MahMah to host them. Those opportunistic fellows would stay at our place, enjoying free food, accommodation and use of the car and driver.

It was Hilda's Miss Mary who helped the Zhang girls to register at an English school, rather than a Chinese school. Another chance happening that could have made our futures very different!

During the 1950s Hilda stayed at the shophouse many times. She was kind to the Zhang children, teaching us to play card games – actually to gamble. Three cards was a favourite. She supplied the money and we were allowed to keep whatever we did not lose.

Hilda

For some strange reason I remember a very ordinary gambling session with Hilda when I was around eleven years of age. My older brother Yeh blurted out that I was scratching my toes. Hilda sent me off to wash my hands. I came back too fast and was accused of not doing it properly and had to go back to wash both hands and feet. That whole evening Yeh had dirty looks from me. If looks could kill Yeh would have been dead!

Hilda would tell us funny jokes and she had a store of guessing games. She was also very kind to Zhang Yu's children, especially shy little Wah. Wah was only one when PaPa died.

In the 1950s Hilda settled in Singapore. I think she was often stretched for funds, but she never failed to give me some cash whenever she saw me. But by 1959 Hilda was no longer rich. She had made all the mistakes. She was over-generous, was cheated, had invested unwisely and her spendthrift habits further depleted her wealth. I took Kit to see her around this time. Although she liked Kit, she felt that I could do better.

When I next visited her she came up with a proposal. She had kept a photograph of me, of course a flattering one with sparkling eyes, in her little house.

Li, aged c. 18 years

A male friend of her daughter had seen it and asked whether I was available.

Hilda, with a serious look, told me to meet him. To give him a try. If I ended up with him I would never have to worry about money, as he belonged to one of the richest families in Singapore. Having been madly in love herself and ending up with such a bitter divorce Hilda knew so much about life. She once said "Kiss one moment, kick another moment." Her love life had ended with physical blows. Much as we liked her, Meng had also warned me that Hilda was very materially minded, so I thought a successful match would mean a big ang pau for her. I told her I was going steady with Kit. She urged me to reconsider. This was someone 10 years older. I would be cherished. Besides, he was not bad looking and was professionally qualified. I firmly said no again.

In August 1966, my mother took Hilda to my house in Kuala Lumpur. Unfortunately, Kit and I were out at a dinner party. I was told she was very happy to see my two boys and to carry my baby girl, who was only a few weeks old. I heard she was in financial difficulties. I wished I had been home and that I had been able to give her some money. I never got to meet up with Hilda again. She suffered a painful death from cancer, penniless, in Singapore in the late 1970s. I think of her with affection – she had always been kind to little Li.

A portrait of Little Miss Mary

Little Miss Mary's fortunes were closely connected to Hilda. Miss Mary was really not that little, but she was called such. She was an Indian girl around four foot nine, with plain features, a thick waistline, broad hips and stocky legs. Her hair was pulled into a thick plait that hung down the back of her neck. Miss Mary had a small gap between her two front teeth, all of which were white and strong, and she smiled often. Her great asset was her knowledge of English. She had secondary education in English, although she did not sit for the senior Cambridge school certificate.

As I later learned, Miss Mary lived with her brother in a wooden hut on a large piece of land next to Hilda's palatial dwelling. She would cast covetous eyes on the beautiful house next door. She often gazed at the two magnificent cars parked in front of the house and the tall, elegant Hilda, who was often seen in the garden with her adopted daughter Rosy. Miss Mary was overjoyed when Hilda waved one day and invited her into the house. Hilda was always friendly and sociable. From the moment Miss Mary stepped into the opulent home she became, one could say, a slave to Hilda. She coached Rosy in English and played with the girl. Miss Mary turned up most days, offering to do whatever errands there were. She was Girl Friday and more! She often stayed for lunch and tea, eating English chocolates, cookies, noodles and meat dishes from Hilda's kitchen. I think Little Miss Mary felt she had found paradise on Earth!

Miss Mary received more goodies when Hilda took her to Zhang Yu's shops. She was asked to drop in regularly to give English coaching to my brother Kwok and sister Meng, and any of the adults who wanted to learn English. She was given lunch and paid for her work. Then there was the bonus of two new dresses from the shop each year. How could life get so good?

Meanwhile, Hilda was getting divorced and short of funds. She would have to return to Hong Kong to sell off the last of her inheritance.

Miss Mary worshipped the ground that Hilda walked on. That was no exaggeration. She offered to sell her piece of prime land to help the stressed Hilda. Hilda could pay her back later on. So Miss Mary sold the land, but neither was the real estate advice nor the timing right, and she received a price poorer than expected. Hilda never paid back the money, instead returning to Hong Kong and squandering the remainder of her inheritance. Miss Mary was also to find that, with Zhang Yu's passing, she was no longer required at the shops. Her connection with the Zhang family ended. Goodbye to the two new dresses each year.

During the years of association with the Zhang family, Miss Mary had picked me up as a sidekick. I was always available, lively and very obedient, so I had seen the dream home of a very rich couple at its best and also at its worst!

In 1959 I saw Miss Mary for the last time in Singapore. Hilda gave a small dinner party for her. My sister Meng was there, brother Kwok too. I brought Kit along. Miss Mary seemed shorter. Her body was thicker and her plait less luxuriant. The gap between her front teeth was still there, but she looked sadder. She pleaded for funds, reminding us that she had been instrumental in getting us an English education. Had coached us in English and done so much to help us. She had sold her shared inheritance with her brother to help Hilda and now they were both destitute. Sister Meng was approached to provide a small stipend. Meng told me that Miss Mary had been paid regularly by PaPa and that we did not owe her anything.

Anyway, that evening we all pulled out some cash. Kit gave Miss Mary $20 from what remained of his $50 monthly allowance, although he later told me he had a bad impression of her. I felt some sympathy for the Miss Mary with whom I had tagged along when I was just a little girl. Goodbye Miss Mary.

2 The world of little Li

Li's birth — my birth — in June 1940 was uneventful. The midwife arrived on time and labour was quick. Jen and Luk May's fifth child came early, without issues. When Luk May had been in labour with her fourth child, Mei, a flying fox had flown through the window and torn the mosquito net. MahMah declared that this was a bad omen and took a dislike to Mei.

There was just one problem with Li: it had been expected, or at least desired, that the fifth child would be a son. Now they had one girl too many. Daughters could be useful sometimes, such as for marriage alliances with business partners. Hopefully, she would turn out to be pretty and strong enough to rear many fine sons. Li was born in the year of the dragon, like her mother, a good year to be born for either boys or girls.

Luk May was healthy enough, although somewhat depleted of calcium after five births, and unable to provide milk for her new baby. Her teeth were starting to suffer, and the low nutrition of wartime did not help. Li, too, was to suffer from poor teeth and bone strength, plus a depressed ribcage. But Luk May passed on to her daughters her good shoulders, suited to cheongsams.

Li turned out to be the runt of the family at five foot two, but cheongsams worked for her too. She also inherited her mother's dimples and broad nose, and later in life uncannily resembled Luk May from certain angles. She got her father's eyes, bright pupils fringed by dark brows. Her father would have preferred those eyes went to Mei, his favourite daughter.

It was impressed on Li from very early that she was Chinese, and, particularly, Shanghainese. She was pleased, considering the Shanghainese to have more class than the Cantonese. When Li studied poetry in school she related to Wordsworth's lyrics on the French Revolution, rewriting it in her mind as: "Bliss was it in that dawn to be alive, but to be Shanghainese was very heaven".

Li was five before she realised who her parents were, for Jen and Luk May lived elsewhere and were addressed as Uncle and

Aunt. Her uncle and aunt were called PaPa and MahMah. Around that time she began to adore her father. Once, on one of the few occasions she was sent to stay with her parents, Li saw them caring for the other children while she was crying in bed. They were treated with love, she thought, but she was not. Did her parents not know she loved them?

When Li was a teenager Jen looked upon her with distaste, never lifting a finger for her. This was to haunt Li her whole life.

I know you never wanted to leave Shanghai, Jen, but did what your father told you to do. You were intended to earn your fortune in Nanyang, enough to help your sisters and parents, then return to Shanghai and die happy in the city of your childhood. You went home in 1947, but needed to keep earning a living in Kuala Lumpur, dreaming of Shanghai. I was the reluctant migrant's daughter.

Love in a traditional Chinese family

Fear and Respect were taught to children in traditional Chinese families. Love was kept silently in the heart. There were no displays of love; touching, hugging and kissing were frowned on. Even young couples in love were discouraged from showing affection in front of their elders. Praise, compliments and encouragement were rare. These were absent in the Zhang family, anyway. Punishment was more the norm, and often Yeh or Li could be found kneeling in front of one of the altars, paying penance for making noise.

Little Li yearned to be touched, to be patted on the head and to be told she was a good girl. There must have been love in the hearts of the adults, but the traditional habits continued. From one generation to the next they were passed on and remained ingrained. I believe things have finally changed in the 21st century.

MahMah was always cold. She never showed any tenderness to her husband. Not even in speech was she gentle to him. But I was lucky, for I saw love in the Zhang household – Zhang Yu embracing Ah Chieh when they thought they were alone. Little Li saw them embrace several times, as the child was everywhere.

I also recall MahMah's attitude towards the display of affection in public. It was around 1950. British soldiers were seen along Batu Road, for there was a milk bar at one end of the road that was popular with the soldiers. Often they walked with an arm around their girlfriends, kissing them. The girls were Eurasian and, occasionally, Chinese. MahMah had seen them and loudly announced her distaste. Should any of the Zhang girls behave in such a manner she would break our legs. She would break our legs even if the male were Chinese!

It had been no better for Kit's father KM, in fact, it was even worse. My father-in-law told me that once, for his misdemeanours, he had to kneel, holding a basin of water over his head. Just as he was about to collapse a shout would come that he might lower the basin.

KM loved his two children, but even he could not break away from the tradition of discipline and punishment. However, it was only his son who "needed" punishment. His daughter was mature and always sensible, almost the perfect child.

Grace dried Kit's tears after being caned. From her there was touching and hugging. She spent time with him in the afternoons when she was home from her teaching job. This bonding was to result in complete trust and belief in his mother, an unshaken faith that lasted a lifetime.

The Chinese traditional belief in discipline also endured in Kit. While he showed tenderness to our daughter, he was strict with our sons. Our second son loved to be hugged, while the older boy hid much within himself. When our second boy was six and Kit saw me hugging him, he told me the boys were growing up and should no longer be hugged, otherwise they would become sissies and effeminate. And the good wife Li did as she was told ...

3 Japanese occupation of Kuala Lumpur

Zhang family recovery

In her first years, while little Li only begins to form lasting memories and is oblivious to anything outside the shophouse, the world collapses around her. World War II is taking place and the Japanese invade Malaya, occupying the country from December 1941 to 1945.

Burning rubber at a Malayan rubber plantation during the British retreat to Singapore, Dec 1941

The Zhang family's faith in the British is to cost them a fortune. The belief that Britain cannot fall and she will protect Singapore led to the decision to flee there. The flight to Singapore had been physically and financially costly with so many children to care for: Kwok was seven, Meng six, Yeh four, Mei two and Li one. Then, just before the war broke out in Malaya, Luk May faithfully delivered her sixth child, a boy named Sang. Singapore was two hundred miles away. They considered taking the maids to help with the children, but there would be nowhere for them to stay.

My sister Meng provided me with the following account at the age of 86. It was a time she could not forget:

"The family left the shops and fled, only to suffer more in Singapore. I vaguely recall that I was given some money in case we got separated. A servant took care of me, and I do not know what happened to the others during that time. We mingled with a huge crowd of refugees, spending one night at an abandoned house. There were air raids, too.

Later, the family reunited and we lived in a remote place, buried away somewhere in jungle-like conditions. There was no piped water, so we used to buy it from a young girl who carried two buckets of water on a pole across her shoulders, until she was raped and killed by Japanese soldiers. That was the first time I set eyes on the Japanese soldiers. They came to our rundown dwellings – looking for women? The maids would hide in the jungle.

Our family even attempted to flee to India by sea, but we seemed to have missed the boat. It was rumoured that a family we were friends with made it to India, though. Once, PaPa was arrested by the Kempeitai for questioning. They accused us of storing up surplus rice stock, not knowing that we had to feed the workers.

When we eventually returned to KL, the shops had been raided and all the valuables taken. Some of those who had stayed behind suffered fewer losses than us."

Only a 99 piece set of green porcelain crockery was saved, as the family had the foresight to pack it away. Li loved the expensive crockery set, which had peacocks on it. It is with my cousin Weng today.

It must have been hard on Zhang Yu to see everything gone. He almost lost his life when he was arrested by the Japanese for questioning. Was it the Kempeitai? Very few Chinese men were released, many never seen again. Every family had someone or knew someone taken away during those days. The Nazis had the Gestapo, the Imperial Japanese had Kempeitai. Not unlike the concentration camps of Nazi Germany, the Imperial Japanese Army had their experimental unit in Harbin, China. Evil men are not limited by nationality.

Yu had to start all over once more, and he did. Slowly, he put his shoulder to the wheel and moved it. The Japanese government in Malaya encouraged business, and by 1943 the Zhang business was on its feet again.

MahMah was her high-spirited self once more. The thought of a junior wife for her husband came up, and she actively went about looking for a suitable candidate.

4 Back to the growing child

The beginning, when I first recall

"A bit further, a bit more, just a bit further" the little three year old with one hand leaning against the wall told herself. She must walk on. She has no further thoughts and no answers.

The hand and fingers are chubby; this child is well fed. She is lucky, for this is 1943, the days of the Second World War, the Japanese occupation of Kuala Lumpur. She has been brought up on canned milk and homemade rice gruel, which she can digest. Her legs are getting stronger.

Every day, she can be found walking alongside the wall. She is always alone. Her mother has had her sixth child, a third son.

Was this my first memory or what Ah Chieh told me? I only know that my earliest memories were of loneliness, of being by myself.

Another day finds Li moving slowly, her hand touching the brickwork. This time an adult hand is placed over the chubby one on the wall. A face appears. The face of a beautiful woman in her twenties, who smiles as she takes the child's hand. The little girl curls her fingers around the adult hand. The round flat face breaks into her first real smile of happiness. Ah Chieh appears in Li's life.

Japanese marching song

Eldest sister Meng runs around the room, screeching in anger. "It's Li again, she annoys me. This time she has stolen my song."

So what is the problem? Last week, Meng came home from school singing a Japanese marching song, moving her legs as if she were marching. She sang it a few times.

"Li has copied me and won't stop singing it. She has stolen my song, so I don't want to sing it anymore," declares a petulant Meng.

In fact, three year old Li has improved on it. With a proud toss of her head and flicking her eyes upward, Li marches forward loudly singing. She is able to sing the whole, albeit short, song, no mean feat for a three year old. Unfortunately, there was no one watching. No one is interested in Li, but Li is learning. She has learned to sing and to move her eyes and her body. Li's memory has demonstrated its ability. A gift that is going to cause her pain, so much pain.

Chinese New Year's Eve

Religion in the Zhang family is a mixture of Confucianism, Buddhism, Taoism, traditional ancestor worship and practicality. Today there is a festive air in the living quarters of the shophouse. It is actually two shophouses, but the wall between them has been demolished on the top level, which accommodates five bedrooms and a very large kitchen. In a similarly large area is an enclosed bathroom. The rest is concreted and used for washing, and there is also a spacious storage area. A sitting room, dining area and even a work area are outside the kitchen.

The five altars have been cleaned. Each has an incense holder sitting in front. Because it is the New Year, a plate of mandarin oranges is sitting there. Mandarins are called gold, as they are thought to bring wealth to the family. Next to the fruit is a small brown cake made of glutinous rice. It is specifically meant to keep the kitchen god's lips sweet and sticky so a good report of this family is given to the gods above.

The kitchen god sits at the entry to the kitchen, the god of wealth a short distance away. In the sitting room, on a raised small wooden board, sits a porcelain statue of Kwan Yin, the goddess of mercy. She is to ensure that mercy is generously shown to this family. Below her sits the earth god, who protects the family.

One of the Zhang family shopfronts, now Batik Rimbun, in 2022. The kitchen was on the top floor, joined to the top floor of shophouse to the left of this one.

    Finally, there is the ancestors' altar, which normally faces a very large open window in the kitchen. Every day it receives five sticks of incense. This is Li's favourite altar.

Little Li wakes early, while it is still dark. She stumbles out of the bedroom. The incense sticks in the urns have all burned, but the air remains filled with their fragrance. The four year old ambles along and bumps into the small table laid before the ancestors' altar. For some reason, the altar had been moved on New Year's Eve to enjoy a more prominent place. Li's eyes widen as she makes out what is on the eight plates before her.

She spies her favourite, the candied lotus seeds, on one of the plates. Slowly, Li sees what is on the others – candied winter melon strips, candied sliced lotus root, candied lemons, red dates, raisins, candied coconut strips and fried puff pastries filled with chopped peanuts, red dates and sugar.

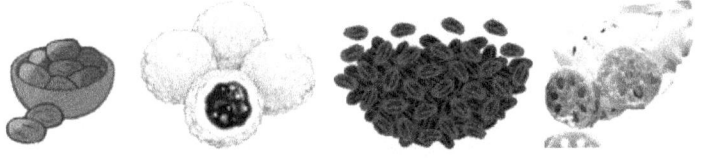

The child crawls onto an upholstered seat by the table. A small chubby hand reaches up to the plate. So many goodies, where to start? It will have to be the candied lotus seeds.

Ten minutes later, and she is still there. There is the sound of smacking lips and a moan of joy escapes from the child. There is a smear of sugar on her nose and on one cheek. The chubby fingers repeatedly run up to the plates, which steadily lose their contents.

"Oh, I love you my ancestors, the candies are all so yummy." She puffs up a bloated tummy, satiated. Li sinks further into the large, upholstered seat, smiles, pouts her lips and closes her eyes. There is gentle breathing – she has fallen asleep.

Later during the Japanese occupation

Food is rationed during the occupation. There is still rice, but supplies are disrupted by the war. PaPa is able to obtain more than some, but not enough. We often have rice mixed with sweet potato. Once, four year old Li is seated for lunch with the other children and Mei knocks over her bowl in a tantrum.

"I do not want stupid potatoes!" she cries.

Luk May scoops up the contents from the bowl and empties the rice from her own bowl into Mei's, which seems to satisfy Mei. Li watches, wide-eyed, not understanding. She has never had a tantrum, not gotten her demands met in such a way.

Another incident involves a Japanese man appearing at the house. He is a doctor, with a friendly but businesslike manner. He has come to check on the newborn, but it turns out to be a scare, as the baby is fine. There is great excitement after his departure. The cupboard door had been left open, with a package of British pound notes inside. PaPa had obtained them for security. However, it was the death penalty for anyone caught in possession of the currency. Ah Chieh had walked over under the pretence of getting a nappy and closed it before the doctor could see it. She is the hero that day.

In mid-1945 the sirens pierce the morning air. Li is at breakfast with Ah Chieh. A big plate of fried sweet potatoes is brought out of the kitchen, still steaming, one of her favourites. By her calculations, Li should get three pieces. Ah Chieh grabs the plate and instructs Li to follow her down to the air raid shelter at the back of the shop, which PaPa had built with the help of the neighbours. All Li wants is the sweet potatoes, so she agrees to follow the plate of them down into the shelter.

The neighbours are already there and clear a space. Li is given what she thinks is the smallest piece on the plate, then Ah Chieh offers the rest around to the neighbours. Li's eyes follow the plate. Soon, the air raid is over and everyone is gone, just as the sweet potatoes are gone. Li feels robbed.

5 New domestic arrangements

Ah Chieh, the young wife

What we were taught to call Ah Chieh was the translation into Cantonese from the Shanghainese for sister. Ah Chieh, I relate your young life story as you told it to me. Your children would love to know.

Ah Chieh grew up in a small village of peasants. Life was simple. At the first rays of sunshine, the cocks would crow and the village would wake. For thousands of years life had gone on much the same. In the good years there was laughter and gongs, bells, drums. In the years of poor harvest there was hunger and death. The simple souls only wished to remember the good years and hoped for more.

Enter Ah Chieh's uncle, a youth eager to sample the pleasures of life, knowing only his own selfish needs. Gambling was a favourite pastime when he could get money. The youth promised young Ah Chieh that he would take her to one of the festivals in the next village, which was bigger and had better shows. Their village was small and few travelling troupes came. If they were lucky a small acrobatic troupe might visit. Or if they got really lucky, an acting troupe would perform sketches from Chinese classics, like Dream of the Red Chamber or Madam White Snake.

One morning, the young girl was piggybacking her one year old sister and doing household chores, their parents in the fields, when uncle appeared. He told her there was a big festival in the next village and they must leave early, otherwise they would not be back by nightfall. Twelve year old Ah Chieh left the baby with a kindly neighbour, promising to be home soon.

Uncle took her to the next village and into a small house, saying he had to visit this lady and then he would take her to the festival. First they would have a snack in the house. They sat down to some glutinous sweet rice balls (tong yuen). Then uncle disappeared and Ah Chieh found herself locked in the house. Something was wrong. Much later Ah Chieh found out that she had been sold to this small foot-bound lady.

Ah Chieh had no way of escaping, no funds, and did not know the way back to her village in any case. She cried for three days. Slowly, Ah Chieh adjusted to her new circumstances and started a new life. She learned to call the lady mother. She trained for the Peking Opera. She learned to sing and dance, then to do acrobatics. She was taught by more than one shifu. She did the washing, sewing and cooking. Gentle soul that she was, Ah Chieh learned to love her new mother.

Ah Chieh's mother also adopted two young girls, sisters for Ah Chieh, and all three came to live with us in Malaya.

I shared a room with Ah Chieh's mother when I was six. I would watch her bind and unbind her feet morning and evening. Only when they were firmly wrapped could she walk.

Ah Chieh, I knew you were beautiful and adored you from the moment I met you when I was three years old. Loving you was to cost me pain and further damage.

You married into the Zhang family when you were in your early twenties. Round eyes, good complexion and cheekbones, a beautiful mouth. You stood about five feet four and had a good figure. From your training, your best act was treading a large plastic ball across a stage. You had juggling tricks: spinning plates on sticks, five or six plates to each hand. I remember you doing a sketch from a Peking Opera play when I was small. You played the wife of a general who needed an imperial edict to open the gates of the city or else the troops could not leave to fight. You pinched the baby to make it cry and manipulated things so you could get the edict.

Apparently MahMah had seen you perform, as she was an opera fan. She approved of you and chose you as a second wife to PaPa, since the couple, in their thirties, had no offspring. You were to give him fine sons. Ah Chieh, why did you choose to be a junior wife to a businessman in his late thirties?

*

Years later, she told me the reason.

World War II was approaching. For China, war started with Japan in 1937 following the Marco Polo Bridge incident, just outside Beijing. The Japanese had been active in Manchuria and made their ambitions all too clear. The news had spread through southeast Asia.

Ah Chieh's concern in life was for her mother and her two adopted younger sisters, Lao Er and Lao San. At this time Ah Chieh was called Lao Da. She was a single lady and needed protection, particularly with the war approaching. Single women were not safe. She had been given the opportunity to meet PaPa and liked what she saw. So, she reasoned, here was an imposing-looking man, perhaps the brightest star in Kuala Lumpur's Shanghainese community. Why not marry him? There were few outstanding Shanghainese men around and he was the best. So what if he was married? His wife was the one pushing for the union. Having two wives was not uncommon in China, especially if the first marriage proved to be barren. Ah Chieh's terms of marriage to PaPa included one cup of good coffee and cigarettes daily for Granny and care for the girls, although Lao Er returned to Shanghai after only a year or so.

Who knew that PaPa would not survive seven years after their marriage?

Life became hard after PaPa's death. The Shanghai Dressmaking Co needed a guiding hand to replace his, and there was none. The various expert tailors left to start new companies of their own, and they did well. There was also a huge debt left by the lavish funeral.

MahMah had taken over the management of the shops, which were quickly going downhill. No new goods or materials were imported. Within a year, the business was no longer profitable. The small amounts of cash PaPa used to hand to Ah

Chieh vanished. Her mother's allowance shrank, and there was not even money to send back to China for the Zhang relatives.

Ah Chieh was still beautiful, and still had friends who liked her company, but social outings were little fun as she had no money to spend. She had three small children. The first two were cared for by the professional Black and White maids, so-called because of their uniforms. Now she had to help look after the youngest. Ma Ma's opium addiction made matters worse. Her foul mouth and mood swings made life a misery for Ah Chieh. Ah Heng suspected that Ah Chieh might be tempted to marry out of the family and shared her concerns with MahMah.

When I was five, I was lonely and cried for Ah Chieh's time. After she first gave birth, I remember hiding next to the chair where she had her special meals. The smell of steamed chicken, ginger soup in white wine with fungus, pig trotters in vinegar with ginger and boiled egg wafted down to me. Secretly, she would feed me many juicy pieces of meat and I developed an appetite for good food.

During the many stolen moments PaPa had with her, I had been there. They only spoke in Shanghainese, which I understood, although I was never encouraged to learn the dialect, and recall many of their conversations. Before I was caned and cursed at, I witnessed their love.

I had been Ah Chieh's little companion, keeping her amused. I remember trishaw rides in the morning to the famous pau (Chinese bun) shop in Kuala Lumpur. Now that she had to care for one of her own children, Ah Chieh had less time for me.

Then in 1951 my heart broke. I came home from school to be told that Ah Chieh had run away with her mother and two younger children. She had gone to Penang to marry a friend of PaPa's and did not intend to come back. The one person who had shown me affection was gone. I crawled into a cupboard and hid for an hour. My despair was such that

I wanted to disappear or die. Of course, nobody looked for me. MahMah had told me countless times that I was a worthless piece of turd.

Ah Chieh was worthless too, I was now told, although nobody could convince me of this. I was sure she had to do what she did to continue to provide for her mother. Night after night I cried for her. Why did she not take me with her? Then I decided to search for her. I was convinced I would see her again.

Kuala Lumpur was not a big place. I knew where her sister lived, as Ah Chieh had taken me there when Lao San was pregnant. I found most of my way there, then enquired until I got directions. The family, several sets of married couples, lived in one big house. I found Lao San. The visit from an eleven year old certainly surprised her. Perhaps she did not know that I had the freedom to roam and that nobody would look for me. Lao San said that Ah Chieh would only return every few months. Accepting this, I asked her to tell me when and where to find Ah Chieh when she returned.

Lao San kept her promise, and later that year I found myself outside a huge house with a big garden. It was early morning, and I was told Ah Chieh was still asleep. I waited in the sitting room for two hours until she came down the stairs. Before she reached the bottom step, I ran to meet her and she gave me that beautiful smile. How I had waited for that smile!

Her husband also had a nice smile, which appeared when he saw me. He gave me a little money on the few times I saw him after then. He certainly helped feed my addiction to candies!

I would visit Ah Chieh a couple of times per year until around 1959, when she moved to Hong Kong. I remember I received presents: three pairs of beautiful earrings and a shawl. It wasn't until the 1970s that I saw her again, when she returned to Kuala Lumpur. Her sons, who had good jobs, asked her to come home where they could look after her. Her daughter had migrated to Australia.

After Kit and I had moved to Sydney with our children in 1977, Ah Chieh's daughter contacted me from Melbourne. Ah Chieh was going to stay with me for a week or so. Kit welcomed her – he knew how important she had been to me, but he would have welcomed her all the same. It was a very joyful holiday. My youngest son, six at the time, devoured her noodles and dumplings. During this time she told me many things about the Zhang family.

Li and Ah Chieh

A few years later, she came to Australia again to spend time with her daughter and grandchildren. She visited me in Sydney twice more, and Kit put up with our loud talking and laughing. The third time, she had aged and had started applying camphor oil to her skin, filling the house with its stench, which Kit found too strong.

When her daughter also came to Sydney during that third holiday, she wore clothes that I had bought for her mother. Clothes I would hesitate to buy for myself I had bought for Ah Chieh. Why did she give them away? Was my love for her so inferior? I was very hurt.

My memory is that those weeks pass slowly. We are not happy as we were during the previous visits. Ah Chieh leaves for Melbourne. I load her with presents. At the airports, she moves through immigration, no hug.

A month later, Ah Chieh rings from Melbourne. She has just learned that my daughter is getting married and wants to attend. I tell her no, the house is too small, Kit's mother is coming, and she has priority. Ah Chieh pleads that she does not mind sleeping on the floor. I am unmoved and refuse. I do not want trouble from Grace, and, subsequently, Kit. Grace was the grandmother, and nobody would be allowed to steal her thunder. I do not see Ah Chieh again. Some years later she passed away.

Ah Chieh, I should have gone to your funeral, but I did not receive the message about your passing. The fault is mine, for I did not keep tabs on you. Even after your second marriage, your life was not easy. In death, you received the peace that life never gave you. I did love you, and I apologise for hurting you. I loved your three children too. It seems that I had the tendency to love, to hug even strangers, but that was before the caning and cursing.

A portrait of Grandma See and foot binding

Grandma PorPor See came into the Zhang family when Ah Chieh married Zhang Yu as a second wife. PorPor is a title given to a grandmother on the mother's side. Chinese children were taught to address all old ladies as PorPor. See was her Chinese surname, and also Ah Chieh's surname.

I only really became aware of PorPor when I was six and shared a bedroom with her for a while. I had many bedrooms as a child, as I was shifted about often.

PorPor must have been in her late fifties, but she always looked old to me. Her hair was drawn back into a bun. She wore a Chinese blouse with a Chinese collar and Chinese cloth buttons that were light blue or grey and a pair of soft Chinese trousers, always black. To me, her face was that of a typical old lady – rather placid and expressionless. However she looked different when she was with her best friend, another old lady who lived down the street, as they often argued and she would look ferocious then. But PorPor had one difference. She had slightly stained brown teeth and her lower teeth were a little crooked. The staining was due to her two loves and luxuries in life, coffee and cigarettes. A good cup of coffee in the early morning followed by a good-quality cigarette made her day. Cheap coffee and self-folded cigarettes were plentiful in Malaya, but PorPor would exclaim that those were not for her. While he lived, son-in-law Yu saw to it that she always had these two commodities.

Little Li watched her morning and evening ritual, always fascinated. PorPor had bound feet and could take only small steps. She was never keen to go out on foot, and since the Zhangs had a car she was able to leave the house. Each morning she had to strap up her feet before she could walk. Out came the rolls of gauze with which she wrapped her deformed toes. Only the big toe was normal. The other four toes had their bones broken. They were loose and floppy and had to be pushed under, into the sole. The gauze had to be wrapped tightly over the loose flesh, a few times round and round. It was like a small bundle with a large, pointed top! Once the strapping was done PorPor would push her feet into especially made cloth shoes. Only then could she stand up and move around. This ritual was reversed before retiring to bed.

As a teenager I used to compare the bound foot to the Chinese speciality of rice wrapped in lotus leaves, tied tightly with string, not quite aware of the blight the foot binding practice was to Chinese women. The ideal age for foot binding was when girls were four to five years, and the latest at nine. This meant it happened to PorPor around the late 1880s.

I learnt that MahMah had also been subjected to foot-binding but had a lucky escape; it stopped before any real damage was done. I remembered that MahMah's little toe looked a bit floppy. She had small feet but she wore normal shoes and walked normally, although slowly. For her it must have happened in the early 1900s, in China of course.

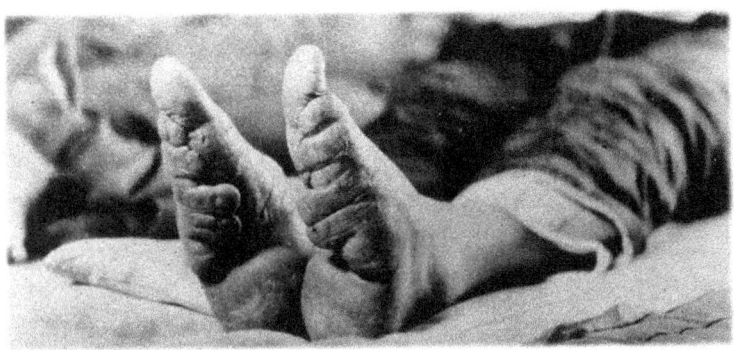

Feet of a Chinese woman, showing the effects of foot-binding

Domestic politics in the Zhang household

A sinister figure appears in the Zhang household when PaPa and Ah Chieh have their first child. A specialist baby amah called Ah Heng, from the Amah sisterhood, professional servants who have their own code of conduct. They are known to be honest and hard-working. They take an oath to remain virgins and unwed, although a few did leave the sisterhood and get married. They have long single plaits and wear long white sleeves and soft black trousers. They are all from Canton, China. Many travel together in small groups, renting a room in the city to which they return between jobs and on rest days. There are rumours that some of them are lesbians, but not Ah Heng.

Ah Heng is hardly five feet tall, with an ordinary demeanour, but there is an intelligent look about her. She is in her early twenties. As time will tell, she is one tough cookie. A good manipulator and quick to exploit any situation that presents itself.

Under her care, the baby Weng is always clean and cute, his cries quickly hushed. Weng is the trump card Ah Heng uses to gain favour with MahMah. Yu becomes aware of her growing influence over MahMah: Ah Heng has convinced her that they must feed the baby herbs and Chinese medicine, including small, pounded pearls. Ah Heng feels it makes the child stable and untroubled by loud sounds. Yu calls this nonsense, causing Ah Heng to threaten to resign. MahMah panics and hurls insults at her husband. Ah Heng stays and rewards MahMah by teaching Weng to smile and gurgle during playtime with MahMah. With Zhang Yu's death, MahMah relies more and more on the baby amah.

Ah Heng has a slashing tongue, calling Ah Chieh a concubine and the children parasites, becoming bolder after PaPa's death. She doesn't know that their grandfather invested much money into the dry cleaning shop, which he co-owned. This was a "Chinaman's agreement", a family understanding never to be disputed.

The Chinaman believes in honour. Should he go back on his word (and he should not), his life will be marked by shame and dishonour. No contract or signature is required to legitimise this understanding; a Chinaman's word is to be trusted. He would feel deeply aggrieved if you do not accept his word. That was the belief at the time.

*

I often went out with Ah Heng. Sometimes she would take me to the temple and I often held the joss sticks. I would kneel in prayer at the altar of the gods. I also had no hesitation in kneeling in a Catholic church when our housemaid Mary took me there. I just loved going out, not caring where, and did as I was told.

I recall one day when Ah Heng told me she had a boyfriend who broke her heart and caused her to join the sisterhood. I do not know whether that was true. I doubted she had a heart, because she was the one who reported the misdemeanours that led to MahMah caning me and Yeh. She disliked Yeh, and the feeling was clearly mutual.

In hindsight, I realised she did have a heart: for baby Weng. She was with him until he was in his thirties and looked after his son. Ah Heng left him involuntarily: she unwisely took on Weng's wife and lost.

From her I learned about Confucius, the Chinese gods and ancestor worship. As Weng grew I was selected as the one to amuse him. Ah Heng organised outings for us to see Chinese movies together. I loved watching the good gods defeat the bad ones in the skies! In the early 1950s I got to enjoy the Cantonese opera. I often dressed in Ah Chieh's old opera costumes, acting out the part of the tragic heroine. Weng would have to be the prince and my cousins the villains or foot soldiers.

When the business went downhill and cash became scarce, the dressmaking shop was leased out as a coffee shop. The Zhang children had no breakfast, beverages, biscuits or toothpaste at that time. But Ah Heng took care to see that Weng was properly fed. When I played with him, I was rewarded with Chinese cookies. Soon enough, Ah Heng was spending her monthly salary on Weng.

Ah Heng and my father did not get along. Once, Jen slapped Weng with his heavy hand, leaving a scar. I had heard the commotion and rushed downstairs to see senior workers holding my father and Weng apart. Weng was reprimanded for crossing his elder. I burst into tears, screaming for everyone not to fight. I knew how rash and unreasonable my father could be and did not want my cousin harmed. Ah Heng also appeared on the scene and began shouting at my father.

"He has had no father since he was five years old and you hurt him?!"

My mother appeared and told Ah Heng to remember her place as an employee. She retorted "I physically brought him up. I feel pain as a mother!"

I feel ashamed of my parents, and feel Weng's pain.

*

For some years I slept in the same room as Ah Heng and Weng. Ah Heng faithfully looked after his needs. She would yell at me, which was common in this household, where children now bore the frustration of the adults. She called me a worm and, worse, Zan Zi Bu, which translates to "provocative and unreasonable female". She eventually stopped using it, but my mother took over, knowing I hated the nickname and used it to taunt me. I guess I had to be her villain too. My mother and Ah Heng disliked each other, with Ah Heng telling me my parents had unhealthy sexual appetites.

Ah Heng also fanned my interest in China. She often consulted a Chinese calendar, which gave advice on almost everything from good days to go to the temple to fasting days and when to travel. This stirred my imagination. I remember the occasion when she brought out her precious postcards depicting the Imperial Palace in Beijing. There was a huge hall with large supporting pillars, an altar, joss sticks in front of a god. I felt mesmerised by them, like I was walking along that hall with cool marble under my bare feet. I could smell the incense of the joss sticks. It was the first time I felt I might have lived another life.

After a few years, I moved to the other end of the building where my siblings slept. I never disliked Ah Heng. I felt she had contributed to my developing mind, which created some kinship between us. I am sorry that she died lonely and that her life had not been easy.

6 More Zhang family memories

Zhang Yu, Ah Chieh and little Li

Zhang Yu was PaPa, the Patriarch. His one life affected so many others, not just my family and his employees. He was always either working or helping the Shanghainese community. I was to learn of this at his funeral, from the many strange faces that came to bid him farewell.

Of the children, I perhaps knew him best because of my close relationship with Ah Chieh. I remember him relaxing in the sitting room after dinner. He would have his cigarette and a tall glass of Chinese tea as he played cards. There was always the occasional cough to be heard after everyone had gone to bed. My bedroom at the time was next to the sitting room, so I could hear the shuffle of cards, the cough and sipping of tea.

There is something strange I can neither explain nor conceal. For many nights after PaPa's death I still heard his nightly routine. Sweating with fear, one night I gathered the courage to look for him. There was nothing but a flickering lamp in front of the large portrait on the altar dedicated to his memory. Three moths would appear most nights, resting on his portrait.

I remember an outing that made me a deliriously happy child. It is early morning, and Ah Chieh calls for me to get ready to go out. She tells me we are going to a Chinese restaurant where they serve the best pau in Kuala Lumpur, in the Central Market next to the Gombak River. A trishaw is hailed. Ah Chieh and PaPa take the cushioned seat and I squat at their feet. I feel joy as the young trishaw rider paddles hard and the vehicle shoots into the street.

I wonder if my love for the cool air dated from this time when I was only about six. The exhilaration I felt when the wind rushed past was the same when, much later, Kit took me out on my first fast motorbike ride.

Back to the breakfast place. Pau is their speciality. There is also glutinous rice and a limited selection of dim sim. Needless to say I enjoy it. Ah Chieh impresses on me that I must be very careful not to let slip to MahMah where we have been, otherwise we will never be able to go out again. You would never have found anyone as obedient as little Li then!

Ah Chieh teaches me to sing songs in Mandarin. I sing the songs, but I do not know the meaning. All I know is that they are sad. There is a plaintive air about them, but I like them. The Zhang women in our household do not speak Mandarin, only Shanghainese amongst themselves and heavily accented Cantonese to the children and servants. They think this way they are able to keep their secrets. They don't realise the children can understand, just lacking the practice to speak Shanghainese well.

Ah Chieh speaks both Mandarin and Shanghainese. She teaches me a Shanghainese ditty about a travelling salesman who carries a little suitcase full of miniature Chinese instruments, such as cymbals, gongs, drums, bells and flutes. When singing, Ah Chieh knocks her elbow and knuckles on the table, creating a certain rhythm. Li is haunted by the ditty and its sadness for the rest of her life. After they marry, Li sings the song to Kit, who knows that it is a sort of sad reverie, and encourages her to sing it as much as she wants.

Yam cakes and a fall down the stairs

Little Li is taught by MahMah that children must not get in the way of adults. That PaPa is always busy working so the family has rice to eat. That Li must keep out of his way. With tenderness Li recalls an episode in late 1945.

Little Li is put to her afternoon nap and sleeps longer than usual. She is just awakening from her sleep when Li hears the maid say that the kitchen has made steamed yam cake (woo tau ko) for afternoon tea. The words yam cake make her sit up. That is her favourite food! But the next words from the maid fill her with dismay. The chubby child is usually at the kitchen door, the first to sample what was produced for afternoon tea. This time, they had forgotten little Li, who had overslept, and Li's siblings had already eaten up everything. However not all was lost, as a plate of the yam cake had been sent down to the shop for Zhang Yu and there could be some left.

Little Li slips on her sandals and hurries to the stairs on a mission in search of the yam cakes. In her haste and still drowsy from sleep, she misses a step at the top of the stairs and hurtles downwards. It is a big fall. A figure materialises at the bottom of the stairs at the right moment and catches her. It is PaPa.

The five year old sobs, with a rapidly heaving chest and big drops of tears rolling down her cheeks, for she is frightened and in shock. Ah Chieh also suddenly appears and rubs her back. Li does not get to see Ah Chieh as often these days. Suddenly the sobbing stops as Li sees a plate of yam cakes moving towards her. There are so many pieces still there, as PaPa has not had time to eat them all. He brings them to her as her eyes glow with happiness. She eats, oh how she eats. How can a small child have such a big appetite! PaPa stands and watches her devour the cakes, and little Li begins to grow attached to him.

A rickshaw ride

Large raindrops pelt the canvas cover of the rickshaw. The vehicle moves awkwardly as the puller grapples with the wet conditions. He shouts to the passengers to stop rocking inside or else the rickshaw will overturn. There are three people inside: a five year old girl, an eight year old boy and housemaid, who is 16. Another rickshaw is carrying more children and another housemaid ahead of them. Li pushes her brother Yeh on the basis that he is squishing her in the middle. The housemaid tells Li that her brother is a boy, so he requires more space. Li disagrees, so the punching and the puller's shouts continue until the housemaid raps Li on the head. The rickshaw steadies at last. Maybe they will get home without a mud bath.

Li turns her anger on the housemaid. "This is the second time you knock me on the head today. I am going to report you to MahMah."

Rickshaw in Singapore, 1941-45

"Don't you dare. I will report you for dirtying your dress yesterday because you sat on the ground. The washerwoman complained and said she will resign." A memory of caning surfaces in Li's mind at the housemaid's words. No more complaints come from Li for the rest of the ride home.

The china doll

Kuala Lumpur is thriving once again and the Zhang family business is doing well. PaPa is busy as ever but cheerful, as he still trusts the British despite their failure to defend Singapore and Malaya against the Japanese. Little Li skips around merrily.

She knows there were hard times and that the adults had been sad. But Li is approaching her sixth birthday in June, and is ever looking for excitement.

Something is happening at the dressmaking shop this morning. The window on the right always displays a wedding dress. It is the only business that makes and rents out western wedding dresses, so popular with the locals. Every two months or so a new model is put on show. Years later, Li's close friend Swee Yin told her that her mother's wedding dress had been made by the Shanghai Dressmaking Co, as that was where one went. Her mother had been the daughter of a rich merchant. But today people are working on the display window on the left. The old items are removed and new ones are brought in.

Little Li stands transfixed, staring at the new items. True, there is a beautiful, sequinned evening cheongsam, but something else holds Li's gaze. She is fascinated by a porcelain blue-eyed doll that sits next to the cheongsam.

Zhang Yu has managed to get some foreign items again. Papa is always so clever and has the contacts. This is an English doll. Little Li is mesmerised. There is joy in her round face and she claps her hands at the sight of it. Li has fallen in love. The doll has blue eyes, pink cheeks, Cupid red lips and brown hair. She wears a pretty frilly dress, white socks and white shoes. It is the most beautiful thing Li has ever seen.

The next few mornings Li is found standing near the display window, eyes focussed on the doll. She is there after her nap and after her dinner before the lights go off and the shop closes.

In her bed Li speaks ever so softly. "Oh my beautiful doll, I will treat you most tenderly. You can rest your head on my pillow. You can have half my bed. I will only sleep at the side. If only I can have you."

But little Li knows that she will never own the doll. She is a nobody. Just the day before she had gotten into MahMah's path while running around as usual. She hoped to bump into Ah Chieh, who, since giving birth to Weng, was not often around. Li sometimes caught sight of her leaving in the family car. MahMah had yelled at Li.

"Get out of my way, you useless thing. Not only are you a big rice eater, for the housemaid has reported that you have a big appetite, must you be a nuisance and get into people's way?"

Li is being looked after by Ah Foong, who scolds and calls her a dirty, smelly girl. Li cries when Ah Foong washes her – always dousing her with cold water.

Little Li cannot recall playing with toys. She never had a doll, not even the cheap plastic ones sold at the local shops. She can only recall hugging her pillow. Nobody could stop her from looking at the blue-eyed doll, but she was not allowed to touch anything in the display windows.

The doll is there no more than a month. One day the wife of the most popular solicitor in Kuala Lumpur comes to the shop with her daughter. The girl sees the doll and asks for it. Ah Chieh, there to serve the VIPs, hands the doll to the mother, saying, "You are one of our good customers. The doll is a gift to your daughter from our shop."

Little Li witnesses it all. Her heart breaks. She runs to the back of the shop as hot tears cascade down her cheeks. She is unimportant. Who would want to give her a doll? For many days, Li stands near the display window, looking at the empty spot where the doll had been. Yes, at five Li knows pain. She also learns acceptance. Li never forgets the blue-eyed doll, but is resilient and moves on.

Caning

It is 2022 in my home in Concord, Sydney. I receive a photo from my sister Meng of herself and me. I was about six years old, now a dark skinny child.

It brought back a flood of very painful memories. The abuse had already begun.

I wept for the three year old Li who wandered in the shophouse with minimal care. I wept for the five year old who was becoming aware of herself. She cried every night, soaking her pillow, for she was lonely and had no one to turn to at night. Li never received any parental love.

Sister Meng and Li, aged 6

The regular caning began from the time she was six. Together with brother Yeh, who was three years older, it was punishment for making noise. He received the big cane and Li the smaller cane. As the caning took place the verbal abuse also started. The two children were told they were good for nothing, should never have been born, that the ancestors had done something wrong. That was the reason for their existence! At best, the boy would end up a robber and the girl a prostitute. This happened every week for the next five years.

The person who meted out the punishment was MahMah, the opium-addicted cousin of the children's father, who acted as their guardian. The person who complained about the noise was Ah Heng, the senior servant of the household. Both women were hard, with no compassion. The children's parents lived elsewhere. They had done their job and given them birth, so that was it. This was the simple scenario; the rest was too complicated.

A bond between the children grew out of the shared misery, although Yeh suffered the most. Their two oldest siblings, Kwok and Meng had been welcomed as the firstborn boy and girl, and were better treated. The other three children, Mei, Sang and Chien, had gone to Singapore with their parents, returning when Li was 13.

I recall, while gazing at the old photo, that life was no easier with the return of Jen and Luk May, who were almost strangers to me and Yeh. As my father would yell at us when we angered him, we did not have the required respect and filial piety. We had been on our own for too long and became independent. Our parents' response was to punish us, especially non-compliant me.

*

A six year old girl and her nine year old brother kneel on the wooden floor, waiting for their punishment. Three feather dusters are on the dining table, the handles acting as the canes. They normally rest below the porcelain statue of Kwan Yin, goddess of mercy. But there was to be no mercy for the two children on their caning day.

A shrill voice rings out. "You worthless pieces of trash! You turds. We only have these two shops. We do not have any other property, no rubber estates. All you know how to do is eat us poor. You robber [to Yeh] and you prostitute [to Li]. My predictions about you two will certainly come true. You are a curse to your parents."

They get the full works that day.

"Sixteen generations ago your ancestors did unspeakably evil deeds. That is why you two were born."

What was their sin? Ah Heng had reported them to MahMah for being naughty again. They had run on the floorboards, brought dirt into the house, squealed, giggled, yelped and generally been too noisy.

The blows rain down on their legs. It is no better if they cover their legs with their hands. Li learns fast and always pleads for mercy, promising to be good even when she has no idea what she did wrong. She hops right before the cane touches her legs and then pretends to be in agony in an effort to minimise the number of strokes.

I see the big cane hit my brother hard, and he winces but does not cry. This inflames MahMah, so she comes down harder. He does not plead for mercy. My heart aches when I recall his stoic behaviour.

Li gets the small cane, and the red marks fade after a day. The red welts on Yeh's legs are visible for days. It is the cursing that is more painful to Li. Repeatedly being told that she will go down the path of prostitution – the worst thing that could be thought of for a girl – and that MahMah would write her name upside down if anything good came out of her, a near impossible feat. How much resistance is left in these two children?

Perhaps MahMah noticed that little Li was becoming pretty. This was when Li was around nine years of age, for the gangly, thin child was growing up. To her swearing and predictions MahMah now added "Yes, you little bitch, you will be good for sleeping with men!"

Li felt she was of little worth, and it was around this time that she found a pin. Li took the pin to the mirror and watched her fingers slide the point across her face. It was painful and a fine line was drawn along Li's skin, marked by a thin trace of blood. No one had ever told her she had a sweet face or lively eyes. There were no compliments in this household. The child Li wanted to hurt herself, better still, scar her face. Fortunately, no scar formed.

The caning sessions went from 1946 to 1951. It was a good day when MahMah was distracted. PaPa's death in 1949 meant a particularly bad year for us. We were taught to stay still and accept our punishment. Afterwards, Yeh would hide in his room, emerging only for meals.

Many years later, sister Meng tells me that we were the scapegoats for any annoyances suffered by the adults.

"Hush, hush, it is only a dream, a nightmare. You are all right" my husband says. He wakes me up and I'm in tears. Even twenty years later, it was one of my recurring nightmares. Kit knew something of my childhood, but there is a great deal I hold back. It was too much to tell.

In the same way, my sister-in-law would wake Yeh from his recurring nightmare. I wonder how she comforted him.

Kit would put an arm around me. His reassuring hand on top of mine, I would go back to sleep, feeling warm, protected, loved.

*

I was shuttled to and from my parents for short periods when I was six or seven. They stayed in a rented house a short distance away. One day in the shop I called out for an adult, wanting them to know I was feeling sick. MahMah appeared, curling her thin lips.

"Stop your whimpering. Don't you know your mother is not able to care for you? That is why you are back at the shop. She has tuberculosis and has been vomiting blood."

*

Now aged seven, Li is allowed to join the adults and older children at lunch. Unfortunately, her chopstick control is still poor. With great force, a pair of chopsticks hits her fingers, which sting with pain. The painful blow has come from MahMah across the table.

"That is for holding your chopsticks like a leper!"

Answering back is a sin, and no one dares help Li now. Her tears run into her bowl as Li pushes the plain rice into her mouth. She does not dare stretch across the table to take meat or vegetables. A few more meals pass before she is brave enough to supplement her rice, before she improves. The trauma remains, regardless, and chopsticks become a new object to regard with fear.

Opium dreams

It seems ironic that, seventy years later, some of the opium apparatus I saw being used during my childhood now sits in my ornament cupboard in Sydney. It is but two feet away from me as I write.

Opium paraphernalia brought by Ah Chieh, plus the pipe purchased by Kit

As I hold the pieces, a dreamlike haze comes over me and I drop the glass lamp component. It has travelled intact from Kuala Lumpur to Sydney, only to be broken now.

The broken opium lamp, Sydney 2022

I recover half an hour later, my mind not in Sydney, but in a room in Kuala Lumpur. I smell the sweet opium that lingers in the shophouse curtains. There is a double bed with a mosquito net, an expensive mat and a large tray with the opium paraphernalia: a skewer to hold the liquid opium, two scrapers to clear the soot from the opium pipes, two wooden attachments for the pipes, and a glass lamp.

Missing are the two beautiful expensive pipes. Where are they?

Again, Ah Chieh played a part. On her first visit to Sydney, she discovered that Kit was intrigued by opium pipes, as he had bought a cheap one from the central market in Kuala Lumpur. She returned home and dug through old belongings, found the skewer, scrapers and other pieces and brought them to us.

As for the beautiful pipes, years earlier, she had wrapped them in newspaper and thrown them away, convinced they were evil. MahMah's addiction had impaired her ability to manage the family business and indirectly brought ruin to the Zhang family fortune.

*

Two little girls eye each other. They were told to play. Jenni has a soft look, enhanced by her good clothes. Li's bright eyes sweep over Jenni, demanding and questioning. She notices that Jenni has beautiful and clearly expensive light blue shoes. They look English-made and Li would die for them. Jenni's dress is pretty, but the shoes are out of this world. In a thin conspiratorial tone, Li says "I will teach you to play smoke-smoke. Follow me."

As Li leads the way to the dark room, the tell-tale smell grows stronger. Li tells Jenni to take off those beautiful blue shoes, lie down on the mat by the tray and observe her. First, Li has to prepare the pipe. She pretends to open the packet of opium and smear some on the skewer, which is then put over the lamp. In reality, the opium would sizzle in the flame and a bubble would form. The bubble had to be pushed into the opening in the wooden bulb, with the middle of the pipe over the lamp. Only then could one puff on the pipe.

Li puffs on the pipe, making loud noises. Then there is silence. Li lowers the pipe back onto the tray, giving a loud sigh. She rolls her eyes up to the ceiling then closes them, a smile spread across her face. She has seen MahMah do this dozens of times. Jenni thinks it is fun.

*

Visiting the cinema across the road is a great joy. The two young boys who handle the tickets always let Li in for free once the show has started. She is allowed to sit on the cheap seats or in the aisle.

No one taught her how to cross the street, so she runs and tests her luck. Once, when she is nine, she decides to close her eyes and run like the wind. A motorcycle whips around the corner and hits her, sliding some yards away. When she can see properly again, her knees and elbows are bleeding. The young rider has dismounted and eyes her. Satisfied that she is able to stand, he jumps back on his bike and scoots off. One of the cinema boys makes his way over, handing her some of the film programs. She accepts them and furiously begins cleaning her arms and legs. Everything hurts and she is shaken, but all she can think about is the caning she will get if there is a trace of blood on her when she gets home.

7 "I love school"

"Absent for 92 days of the school year. Refuses to do work in class. Always sleepy. To be retained in the same class next year. Promotion not recommended." Sister Meng reads out Li's first year school report.

Li was the youngest in her first year of school so she is no older than those in the new class. While Meng feels ashamed for Li, Li continues to skip school when she can get Ah Chieh's support. Meng has tried her best. She drags Li from bed, but Li runs off to Ah Chieh saying she is sick, for this is her usual ruse. Ah Chieh feels sorry for the six year old and tells eleven year old Meng to leave her at home. Meng gives up. She would end up being late for school with her attempts to get Li dressed and breakfasted. Li says "I hate school" and gleefully runs back to bed. "Why should I go to school, the bed is my best friend."

Three years later the scenario changes. Li announces "I love school, I don't like weekends." Li has started to find school fun!

Li can sing louder than anyone else in her class. She picks up the latest pop songs and sings them during lessons. It is a pity she does not have a good voice. Li laughs the loudest. She is the fastest runner in class, loves to compete, loves athletics.

When Li turns twelve she is selected for the school house team, running with the seventeen year olds from Form Five. She enjoys the weekly physical education class. She can do the splits, the backward bends and the high kicks. Then, in Form Three, there is a folk dancing class, and Li learns the Figure of Eight, Irish Polka, Scottish Jig and the Waltz. Li loves the dancing.

However, Li's running career comes to a sad end. Cooked breakfast home is no more. MahMah is often in an opium haze and no longer checks on breakfast. Senior servant Ah Heng turns a blind eye. She has no love for the Zhang children and has too much to do. With nothing in her stomach to sustain her, Li finds herself sick at the far end of the school field, bent over vomiting after each exertion. It is no fun running anymore!

Meanwhile, Li has been best friends with every single one of her 40 classmates. She quickly discards one and picks up another. But Li has a secret. It is not that she is frivolous. Li is looking for something, something her little friends cannot give her. Li wants the love and attention she is missing at home.

By the age of 14 Li knows she has psychiatric problems. She realises that her behaviour, her constant search for affection, is not quite normal. She is frightened and wonders whether she will be able to find a soul mate. She knows she can love, but will there be someone who reciprocates? Is she lovable?

Li loves her school. It is small, but has both primary and secondary classes, although only one for each grade. Li is popular, for she is spirited and friendly. She is willing to speak up and often volunteers to do things for the teachers. She adores her headmistress and deputy, both English ladies. They are missionaries and dedicated teachers. Li enjoys her classes, but her learning depends on her emotions. She does well in subjects where she admires her teachers. She does not like the teacher who introduces the new subjects in Form Three, algebra and geometry, and switches off, daydreaming, to her detriment. Li is hopeless in art: rich in imagination, but her drawings are fit for the trash can rather than for hanging on the wall.

Li the student is also naive. She gets into trouble with Miss Yzelman, the conservative, no-nonsense teacher. Miss Yzelman takes the senior classes for their weekly singing lessons. One day she asks Li's class whether they would like to make a request. Li thinks of something other than the usual bland songs.

"La Marseillaise", she calls out. Miss Yzelman is furious for some reason and orders Li to stand on the stage, in front of everyone, as punishment. She takes a dislike to Li. Some weeks later Miss Yzelman again asks if anyone would like to make a request. Again Li calls out "La Marseillaise", and again Li is ordered to stand on the stage.

Li does not intend to irritate the teacher. She just wants to sing something more exciting.

8 Reinstatement of British rule

More young migrant workers

Back in the family business, 1946 had similarities to 1933. PaPa managed to bring new workers to Kuala Lumpur. His brief return to China also saw to the successful reorganisation of the Shanghai side of the business.

At the end of the year three Shanghainese migrant boys arrived in Kuala Lumpur. Two fourteen year olds, Ching and Ah Tse, and Sar, who was sixteen. Ching was to be an apprentice for the dressmaking shop and the other two for the dry cleaning shop, the decision made for them by their elders. They accepted their fate. Often, the decision to send a boy-child away simply meant one less mouth to feed in a poor family. But sometimes there was a remote chance that the one sent would save the family by sending money back to their remote village.

Most of the apprentices' salary was remitted to their families in Shanghai by Yu and later Jen. When they were adults their monthly salaries were handed to them. They would then send what they themselves wished.

There was much trepidation, but these three looked forward to some adventure from their new lives away from China. Then again, they hoped to return to their motherland one day with their fortunes from Nanyang.

I remember Ching well. He had big intelligent eyes, was clever and had imagination. He was of average height, with a handsome face and a cheerful look at all times. Ching was one of the boys who carried food from the kitchen but became a shifu at western dress. He learnt English and was able to communicate with his Western clients. It was little wonder that he did well.

I remember he would tease me when I walked past his work area when I was about ten years old. He would call out "Hello my darling" and my reaction was always "I am not your darling!" I would stamp my feet in annoyance. He would laugh and I would run away. I thought he liked us Zhang sisters, especially my eldest sister. He was too smart to entertain any thought of a future with one of us. We were the boss's daughters, and he an employee.

Ching married a pretty seamstress and they lived on the shophouse premises in a large room on the middle floor. I remember his first child, an absolutely adorable girl with big eyes like Ching's. I watched him guiding this child as she learnt to walk. He had a towel around her waist, holding on to it while she toddled along. Some two years later she caught polio and died. He was inconsolable.

Ching made beautiful clothes and inevitably he moved out to start his own business. In my late teens, I went to his new premises, as I loved his clothes, which were always a cut above all the others.

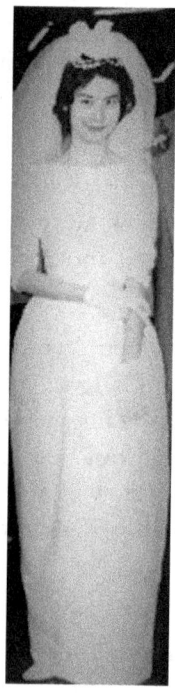

I went back to him for my wedding dress, an off-white duchess satin. He did a beautiful job. He refused payment. Ching also refused payment for my sister Meng's wedding dress. Such was the loyalty of these people. The link is there forever. I still have my wedding dress. I want it cremated with me.

Ching could have retired to Shanghai, but he chose to stay. He also chose to work past his retirement age, his work ethic being such. Ching did not know how to stop.

The oldest of the three boys was Sar. He was tall, broad shouldered, a gentle giant with a ruddy complexion, rather small eyes and a ready smile. He worked at the Oriental International Company, the dry cleaning shop, washing the clothes. When there were carpets for cleaning he would wash them too. Sar was a distant relative of PaPa and was like an uncle to me.

In my early teens I discovered Sar's secret romance after he came out from the work area to the reception area a few times. It was to see Miss Huang, the tall and pretty receptionist. One day I heard him asking her to marry him. Her reply was in the negative. She felt there was no future in marrying a washer. He would not be able to give her much in the way of luxury. His ability to do invisible mending would bring in a bit more money, but still not enough. He would be a good husband, but they would always remain poor. She felt she could do better. Indeed, half a year later she left for a better job. I felt sad that the romance did not blossom.

Some years later Sar saved enough to buy a motorbike. I was nearly sixteen and a few times I asked Sar to give me a ride to Ching's tailoring shop to pick up a new dress. He never refused. I was so shy I would only touch one of his shoulders for balance when he went around a corner. The understanding was that the boss's daughters and employees always kept their distance, and I was so much younger. Sar, the perfect gentleman, did marry. I heard that he was introduced to a local Chinese girl with whom he had many daughters and finally a son. I heard, too, that he brought his mother out from China and kept her busy and happy looking after his many children. He had a good marriage, although they were never wealthy.

The third young migrant was Ah Tse. He was always full of life and mischief. To little Li he looked as if he never washed his face, which was dark and spotty. Ah Tse would carry food down from the kitchen. He was a fast mover and a fast eater. The senior workers had first go at the meals, so Ah Tse ate during the second sitting. Watching them eat was "show time" for me and brother Yeh, two pesky kids. We sat on the stairway, directly above the workers' dining table – first class seats! Brother Yeh admired Ah Tse and named him Mr Flying Chopsticks, as he always managed to grab the last few bits of meat and vegetables.

Ah Tse was also good at games. He was the champion at knocking down cards, a popular game then. Yeh loved watching him play. In addition, he could play the mouth organ, the first I ever heard. He only played Chinese tunes.

Ah Tse was an apprentice at ironing and turned out to be good at the job. He slept on a canvas bed a short distance from where he worked.

He was always cheerful and lively, but one day Ah Tse's mischief went too far. I was around ten years old, often running between the two shops, watching the workers at their jobs. He tried to frighten me away, threatening by moving his iron about. I did not move and he miscalculated, moved his iron too close and the tip touched my arm. I cried out in pain and ran off. My father was at work in the shop and Ah Tse was sent for. I had a minor burn. Ah Tse was clever with words. He convinced my father that I had run into him! There was a scar left behind on my arm, a darkish stain with the outline of the pointed tip of the heavy iron. I learnt to stay a good distance from Ah Tse.

There was something else that Ah Tse did that I could not resist watching. Often clothes needed to be sprayed to get the smoothest results. The ironer could rinse out his mouth, take a huge gulp of water and, using mouth control, spray the garment. Ah Tse was the best. His spray was even and fine. This type of spraying was for trousers and coloured clothes of a heavier texture. I loved watching the human sprayer at work.

Ah Tse followed my father to Singapore when Jen started his small dry cleaning business there. He followed Jen back in 1953 when MahMah made an urgent call for Jen to return to Kuala Lumpur to help manage the shops.

Although he never seemed interested in girls, Ah Tse did marry. It was to a pretty girl of southern Chinese descent. She had come to do washing at the dry cleaning shop. He approached my father for funds for his wedding, as Jen was the closest person to him. I heard that at his wedding two Shanghainese seniors got drunk and quarrelled. When Ah Tse intervened he was accidentally punched hard. Poor Ah Tse!

Ah Tse stayed with the dry cleaning shop until the end and became unemployed. There was no compensation for him when the business folded. He ended up working for his father-in-law, who ran a small dry cleaning business. Ah Tse did the washing and ironing. Ironing was all he knew, for he had little education and few opportunities in life. Workers with only one skill like him faced bleak futures. Zhang Yu would have helped, but his death so many years before meant a hard life for some of these young workers of yesteryear!

None of these three young migrants went back to China to find Shanghainese brides. Neither did my mother's three sons. Nor did her daughters marry Shanghainese men. There was no Zhang Yu to organise trips to China to find a spouse and the Shanghainese community in Malaya was too small.

The Zhang family business

Both the shops were now well staffed. The three young migrants fitted in well and were soon hard at work. In 1947 Zhang Yu also recruited some local Chinese seamstresses to work under the direction of the Shanghainese shifu. PaPa was strict, his standards were high, but he paid well.

Yu must have been a master tailor, for he seemed to know so much about clothes. I often saw him with a tape measure round his neck, although never cutting cloth himself. I remember three incidents that he managed with aplomb. There would have been many others I did not see.

The first was when an English lady with sad eyes and a downcast demeanour came to the shop. She asked to see the boss and Yu appeared. The lady had brought a dress pattern and a piece of material from England, which she showed him. She said she wanted the cloth used to make the dress, that she knew the material might not be quite sufficient, and that was why she needed a top tailor. She was willing to pay.

Yu sent for his top western clothes shifu. The experienced tailor emerged with a tape measure. He took the measurements of the lady and the piece of material she brought. He looked serious, and slowly shook his head. Unfortunately, the material was just some two inches short. Zhang Yu looked at the pattern, turned the piece of material around and spoke to the tailor in Shanghainese.

"If you cut the cloth at this angle, you should be able to do it."

The shifu's small eyes lit up, a smile spread across his face and his high cheek bones became even more pronounced. He waved his cigarette-stained fingers in agreement. Yes, if he cut the cloth at the angle his boss suggested, it could be done.

The second incident is embedded in my memory. I could not have been more than eight years of age and was most impressed by PaPa. He had the skills of a shifu, but he also had the brains of a businessman and could manage people.

A shrill voice echoed through the rooms of the dry cleaning shop. "You stupid man, you have ruined my expensive ball gown."

Mr Wong, the senior clerk at OIC and Ha, senior ironer, were trying to pacify a tall, thin English lady, the wife of a British officer. She kept on screaming and Yu had to be sent for.

Yu arrived and learnt what the problem was. The sleeves of her gown were no longer puffed up. They had collapsed. Ha shifu quietly said in Shanghainese that the material was inferior. After the first wash it was always going to be like that. He had done his best with the ironing. The lady continued to yell. Yu signalled silence, asking her to follow him as he made his way through the opening into the Dressmaking Shop. He was able to quieten her and got her seated.

Yu walked to where his rolls of materials were kept, behind a glass showcase. He selected a few and carried them over to the English lady. These were some of his best materials, light expensive fabrics meant for evening dresses. He sent for the western evening dress shifu to measure the lady and handed her the latest fashion publications.

Yu turned to face her and in simple English said "Choose your pattern, tell the tailor what you want. It will be ready in five days. No charge." With that, Yu left to attend to his other duties.

It seemed to me that the army officer's wife with the hollow cheeks almost collapsed with joy and disbelief. I'm sure she recognised the expensive materials and was going to get the best gown she ever had in her life, made by the top tailor in Kuala Lumpur, thus Malaya, without paying a cent. She was also told she could take her dry cleaned gown home, again with no charge.

This was Zhang Yu's style which little Li would never forget. No penny pinching. Little Li was so proud of him, often wanting to run up to him and hug his legs. She liked the smell of him. But little Li was being made. She had been taught to control her emotions and so she did.

The third incident involved Wei, PaPa's second son, who was only three. He had escaped from the maid and run into the shop as a French lady was being measured for a new dress. Yu was there, as Europeans were VIP customers. The cheeky little boy, who had learnt to say "hello", picked up the hem of the lady's long skirt and said hello to her legs! Then he quickly dropped the hem. The lady was of course surprised. Yu quickly apologised and turned to a worker to send for coffee and cakes from the nearby coffee shop.

A short while later the small group was seated around a table in the Shanghai Dressmaking Co: Yu, his assistant, and a laughing lively French lady, enjoying their coffee. The lady had a good sense of humour and Yu had the charm and ability to deal with every awkward situation. That evening I heard Ah Chieh and PaPa referring to the incident with much amusement.

Those years after the war were good years. The two businesses hummed along, as did the sewing machines at the Shanghai Dressmaking Co.

OIC was doing very well too. The Zhangs' timing had been excellent: the members of the British Army needed someone to keep their uniforms and western suits immaculate. The Army may have its own cleaning department, but still the clothes found their way to OIC. The curtains and carpets of the top officials and the administrators also needed to be kept clean, and OIC could certainly cope with the work.

Jen was often on duty in OIC in those days. His father had trained him, and he had a good knowledge of fabrics, of their delicacy, of shrinkage. He knew the cleaning agents, the dyes and the bleaches. On rare occasions items had to be refused treatment due to their fragility or age. The business had to be protected. Compensation would eat into profits. Jen was there to be consulted and provide advice to the workmen when necessary.

And Li developed a hidden talent. From her childhood years of observing the workers at the dry cleaning shop, adult Li could iron beautifully. Kit's clothes, the boys' clothes and our daughter's frilly dresses and puffed sleeves were all well laundered and presented. Ironing was never a chore. My father never knew there was a daughter interested in the family business – the reluctant migrant's daughter. My grandfather had passed his knowledge to his son, and I learnt from observing the work of the adult migrants around me.

The radio

In 1949, mounted against the wall in the work area of the Shanghai Dressmaking Co, is a radio. A small monthly subscription is paid for its use. The radio station broadcasts news, but only once every morning. Most of the time it plays songs in Mandarin. It is called Rediffusion.

There is an hour of storytelling each day at 6pm, often about the exploits of the Chinese heroes in the early twentieth century, such as the tales of Wong Fei-hung. The Chinese population in Kuala Lumpur is largely of southern Chinese descent, so the broadcast is in Cantonese.

The radio is never turned off. Ah Chieh allows Little Li to be up at all sorts of odd hours – the reason why she is always tired at school – so Li often hears God Save the King played at the station's midnight close.

Sundays are special, for there is an hour-long program in Shanghainese. MahMah comes down to listen. She laughs away, not something that happens often. The other times she laughs are when she plays with baby Weng. The radio announcer calls out "nose" in the Shanghainese dialect, followed by the English word. That is followed by eyes, ears, face, mouth, and so on. MahMah finds it funny. Next is a Shanghainese song – I remember The Good Mother. Other times a poem is recited, accompanied by a clicking sound made by a Chinese instrument, not unlike that of a castanet. The program appeals to the Shanghainese workers, and every Sunday they are found listening eagerly.

Li listens to the Mandarin songs with the migrant workers. They seem to share a certain sense of community.

A favourite of the workers is actress and singer Bai Kwong. In 1950, Bai Kwong visits Kuala Lumpur. She is introduced to Ah Chieh, who still has theatre contacts. Li gets to meet the actress and has a photo taken with her.

Li and Bai Kwong, 1950

9 My siblings

My siblings gave me much joy during my growing years in an environment that was far from happy. I was the smallest child and also the silent observer. In a place where there were no displays of affection or words of love, little Li gave her love to her siblings quietly in her heart.

Brother Kwok - shattered dreams?

Brother Kwok was welcomed into the world with joy in 1933, a male child. He was the firstborn of Jen and Luk May, the start of a new generation. Although he was born outside of Shanghai, the Zhang family line would continue; the blessing had arrived. It had already been decided that he would address Zhang Yu as PaPa and Foong Ying as MahMah.

MahMah was delighted with the new baby. She was infertile, but Luk May was there to do the producing, so all was well! There was a young prince and the domestic staff were made aware of it. The baby and the mother's needs were to be given priority. Brother Kwok seemed destined for a great future.

How was the child to be brought up? MahMah took over completely. PaPa's role was the quiet bystander. After all, the child came from MahMah's side of the family; Jen was her father's nephew.

PaPa was always busy running the shops. He liked looking at the sleeping child but his wife made it clear that she was in charge. She wanted no input from him. Anything he said was regarded as criticism. She was delighted to fuss over the child, and he was spared her querulous nature, so it was in his interests to stay quiet. To provoke her by interfering would lead to swearing and cursing, or worse still, her habit of throwing things and finally taunting him that the position he now enjoyed was due to her father's money.

MahMah allowed Kwok to do as he pleased, for she doted on him. But what did Kwok really have in the way of love and nurturing? MahMah filled his head with false dreams. Over the years she bragged to him that he came from a well-to-do business family and their social standing was at the top of the Shanghainese community. The Zhangs were significant and respected people. She was full of self-importance and her regular boasting filled the child with the same.

The growing boy needed a father figure. Because of MahMah's attitude and temper, PaPa's attempts at discipline failed. Kwok's own father, Jen, had abdicated his role when the child was born and stayed in the background. He gave little thought to his responsibilities as a father. Jen behaved the same way later with Yeh. There was no guidance, no effort, no love. In return, Kwok had neither love nor respect for Jen.

By the time onlooker Li was almost ten, her teenage brother Kwok was a hero. A handsome boy, he had the Zhang eyes and dark eyebrows. He also had the height, slim build and a gracefulness Jen never had. To little Li he was the best looking boy in the whole world. (Was she influenced by the 20 cents he generously paid her to clean his shoes?)

However, with Yu's death in 1949, the Zhang family's social standing, wealth and importance went downhill. At the crucial age of 16, brother Kwok was left rudderless. The one person he respected was gone. Although PaPa had not been close to him he was always reassuringly there. Now he was gone.

Life became cruel for Kwok. MahMah's attention was increasingly turned to little Weng, the son of PaPa and Ah Chieh. Kwok had no one to turn to. Some of his friends had gone to college in Melbourne, Australia, to finish high school and matriculate, so he pestered MahMah and Jen to do the same. Kwok was hoping to become an architect. There were also rumours that the government was going to introduce the compulsory recruitment of youths into the Malayan army. To the Chinese a soldier was at the bottom of the social scale! The Zhang family did not want Kwok in the army. MahMah raised the fare, but no provision was made for his maintenance in Melbourne.

Once out of sight, Kwok seemed to be forgotten. MahMah had little Weng to entertain her and opium sessions to make life worth living. Kwok found himself without winter clothes and no regular allowance, and Melbourne was lonely and cold. For a while Kwok found work as a postman during the long school breaks. On more than one occasion a good friend helped him pay his rent.

A spoilt child, Kwok had not developed good study habits. He forced himself to do his schoolwork, but it seemed too late. Anyway, how do you study when you cannot afford to feed yourself properly? Father Jen found himself landed with the dilemma, as MahMah declared that Kwok was his child, thus his problem! Jen sent some money, but did not realise that Melbourne was a very expensive place by Malayan standards. What he sent was on an irregular basis and vastly inadequate. Soon, Kwok was back in Malaya, junior draughtsman at an architectural firm, working for a pittance.

But love came to Kwok's rescue. He found redemption with a primary school teacher, an uncomplicated soul who was completely devoted to him. They raised three beautiful children together. Through thrift they were able to send all three to university in Melbourne. The eldest fulfilled her father's ambition, becoming an architect.

Kwok did have one weakness: he loved horse racing. Each Saturday he would go to the races, yet showed unbelievable control, placing the lowest of bets, and only on three out of seven races. Thus he turned out to be a winner! Had he shown this trait earlier as a student, I have no doubt he would have easily graduated.

After Kwok's wife passed away he devoted his time to his two grandsons. He found joy in watching them grow. He slept the sleep of those at peace with the world. Kwok passed away in 2019, only months after Kit. I consider his life to be one of success.

Sister Meng

In August 1935 Luk May dutifully produced a second child. It was a girl. Sister Meng had arrived. There was already a male child, so Meng was acceptable.

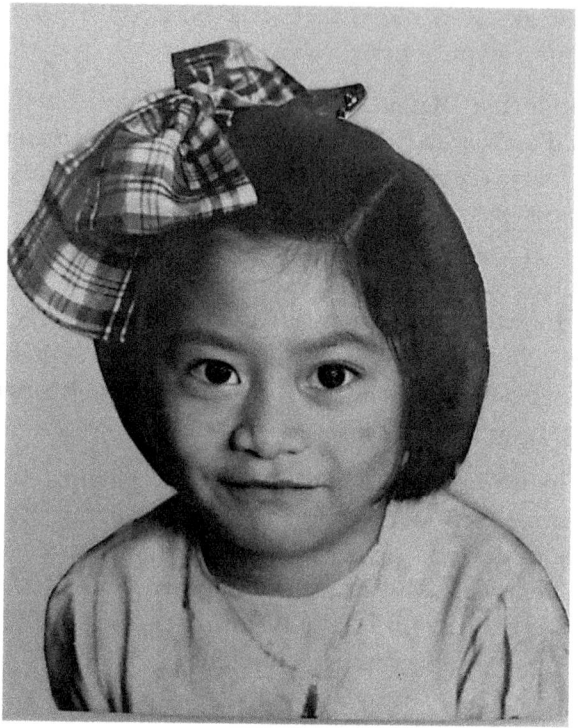

Meng aged 6 or 7

The business was growing steadily. Life was good. Soon the pair of children were running about with a nursemaid behind. Kwok initially had his own exclusive nursemaid, but once Meng started to walk the new, more expensive servant seemed capable of managing both. Meng was a very good, happy child, and needed much less attention than Kwok. By this time, Hilda was a regular at the dressmaking shop, having her clothes done. She had become a good friend to MahMah. Young Kwok and Meng were often found running and laughing in Hilda's large garden, a better place to play in than the shophouses.

Meng was always obedient, and was submissive to Kwok from early in life. She knew that Kwok could do no wrong in MahMah's eyes, and she learnt not to complain.

I have seen so many photos of a laughing Meng, a bright cheerful child. She had the large Zhang eyes and dark eyebrows and our mother's deep dimples. I do not believe I have seen many children as pretty and happy as she. In the photos she always wore lovely dresses and had ribbons in her hair. When Meng smiled she showed her bright beautiful teeth.

PaPa had a soft spot for Meng. Once, when MahMah had picked on her, he had come to the rescue. A quarrel ensued and there was the usual throwing of things by MahMah. Meng was frightened and in tears. After PaPa died Meng was picked on more, as were Yeh and little Li. MahMah missed her husband terribly and vented her frustration on the children.

Meng became shy and timid. She was always serious and loved reading. When she was about 15 years old I saw her in tears. MahMah had found her huddled over a book, which for some reason annoyed her. MahMah yelled at Meng to put away the book and to get a broom instead to sweep out the shop. This was unnecessary, as there were workers to do that. But that was MahMah, and I was also to be subjected to those demands soon enough.

On that occasion Meng had spoken up. She timidly protested that she had exams the next day. That infuriated MahMah, who shouted "Are your studying for the imperial exams?"

This referred to the time-honoured imperial examinations in China when the top officials for the bureaucracy were selected through examinations opened to the brightest students across the kingdom. Meng put down the book, walked to the back of the shop and picked up a broom. She could hardly see what she was sweeping as large drops of tears fell.

I often wonder at the ironies of life. Many years later in Australia, when I went back to university to do Chinese Studies, I chose The Chinese Imperial Examinations as my essay topic. I was absolutely delighted to receive top marks for that essay. It sits in my study today.

I believe that Meng was short-changed. From a vibrant, attractive child she became shy and withdrawn. The type of upbringing we had was just too intimidating for her. But I am glad to say that Meng's kind nature was not crushed. She remained a good daughter and was always generous with her money.

As a child I was always looking for Meng. Mei was closer to me in age, but she lived with our parents and two younger siblings. They were usually in a different house or in Shanghai or Singapore. Yeh would not play with me when there were other boys around. Being five years younger I was not ideal company for Meng. A neighbour and fellow Shanghainese of her own age, May Ling, was always first preference, but Meng would play with me when no one else was around. Little Li made do with crumbs rather than nothing.

My interest in reading might have been encouraged by Meng's example. I remember the occasion when Meng was trying to read Charles Dickens' *Little Dorrit* and I was jumping around her. At close range she flung the thick book at me. It found my head. I became groggy and was quiet for the rest of the day. I do not know what damage the book sustained, but I believe I came off better than the book. Did the incident influence me to read Nicholas Nickleby, The Pickwick Papers and Oliver Twist some years later? I enjoyed them so much.

When Meng reached Fourth Form she convinced MahMah to allow her to go to boarding school in Singapore, paid for by Hilda, who owed MahMah money. Meng made a wise move, in fact, a master move. PaPa was gone, MahMah was unpredictable, and there was every possibility that Meng would not be allowed to finish school. Li was sad – it was lonely without an elder sister to torture!

My second brother, Yeh

The two pieces of thrash get their weekly punishment. Cry, my brother, cry! Why do you stand still and receive the caning in silence? I feel your pain. The blows will continue to rain down on you because you annoy MahMah with your silence. Cry, please cry, you are causing this six year old agony!

Yeh has a beautiful face and exquisite dark eyebrows that taper naturally. We have similar eyes, but Yeh has long eyelashes and also our father's small high western-looking nose. There is a gentleness about Yeh. Despite the harsh childhood, Yeh remains kind and principled.

I share much in common with Yeh. He has never complained, but I know his past haunts him. I caught him in an unguarded moment some years ago when a flash of pain shot across his face. I had innocently referred to an incident in our childhood and it must have brought back bad memories.

Our resemblance is so strong, except for our noses. It used to amuse Yeh's students and colleagues when we worked in the same school. I was there for six weeks of teaching practice, as I was doing my diploma in education. Your deputy headmaster jokingly suggested that we should put on an item dressed as twins at the annual school concert as a treat for the students and teachers!

Our eldest brother shot up in height, but Yeh did not. I felt I knew why: his ill-treatment when he was growing. He did not receive the nourishment or the activity he needed. Our black and white amah, Ah Heng, who was now housekeeper, complained incessantly about his appetite, that he ate too much. I think that was a curb to his food intake. What were our meals like? It was largely rice, mince pork with gravy and a bland soup. It was at this time that he shut himself in his room, no longer going out to play in the back streets with his friends. The growing boy needed food and exercise! He remained small in stature. He was robbed!

Jen and six of his children in 1953. Li is third from the right, Yeh is standing at the back

Yeh had been the leader of the backstreet gang of boys at thirteen. He could organise and had leadership qualities. He was smarter, and could spin the top faster, than anyone else. He could fling his top onto other tops and take chips off them. The spiders that he caught became the champions in the spider fighting competitions. I know because I was there. I was the trusty assistant who held the little box, the home for the newly caught spiders. I helped to find the flies the spiders fed on. I was there when he hunted for spiders at the hedges. I knew what he meant when he exclaimed "na bo peek" when he released a spider. It meant female, so it was no good for fighting!

Sometimes Yeh and I would fly kites. I would be allowed to hold the kite while he ran ahead with the string to catch the wind. Then he would shout to me to release the kite as the wind came up. Other times the kite flopped into the potted holes in the back lane, as there was not enough wind. We would return home with downcast eyes and a damaged kite.

We stopped playing together when Yeh shut himself in his room. His friends were calling for him and I kept telling him they were there, but Yeh would not budge. Was it because of the welts on his legs? He would not tell me. I was a girl and could not be trusted, I might blab.

Our parents did not take to Yeh or to me. We were strangers to them as they were to us. Yeh was 16 and I was 13 when they moved back from Singapore into the dressmaking shop premises. We stayed on the top floor of the shophouse, continued with our lives as before and had little interaction with them. They seldom came up, seldom spoke to us. They would call out to sister Meng to go out to supper with them. We were not included. We continued to be outcasts.

Yeh would often stay in his room studying. Many of our classmates were receiving private tuition, particularly the well-to-do students. Yeh did not read as much and could do with English tutoring, but felt it was useless to ask. We did not receive any encouragement from our parents. Their attitude was "we have given you birth, what more do you want?"

My memory is clear. Quietly, Yeh decides to go on to sixth form. He is always studying. He is good in science and maths. He shows no interest in girls. The only girl he called cute is my friend Dee. She is my playmate, neighbour and fellow Shanghainese. Dee's mother likes Yeh, but at that stage we are only teenagers. Dee is sent overseas to study and our paths do not cross again.

Yeh is in Upper Sixth Form when I am in Lower Sixth Form – he had started school later than he should have because of the war and the disorganisation of the schooling system in its aftermath. While he engages in quiet study I have a great time. Yeh does well in the Higher School Certificate examination and wants to do a science degree. Some of his classmates who did not do as well go for medical studies. Yeh seems humble and unambitious.

Yeh falls on his knees in tears. He is begging Jen for financial support for the science course. He swears he will pay it back by supporting younger brother Sang through university. Jen declares unabashedly "My money is for Sang, for his Chinese University education. You English educated children have no filial piety, unlike the Chinese educated. You do not deserve tertiary education."

Yeh continues to plead. Days later Jen finally agrees.

Our father had initially failed to do his sums. Fees are very reasonable when the student stays home, with only bus fares and lunch to worry about. Yeh has always been frugal. He spends the minimum on clothes and food. His room is the smallest in the house, meant for domestic staff. It can hold no more than a small bed, a desk and a chair. The better rooms upstairs are for the favoured children.

Yeh graduates, the only one in the Zhang household so far, and becomes a teacher, but there is no rejoicing.

Yeh works very hard and is loved by his students. He becomes chemistry master at his cherished school. Then a misunderstanding arises with the principal. A hot tempered Yeh resigns. He is approached to withdraw his resignation. He is too proud and stubborn and leaves even when it breaks his heart to do so.

The fortunate outcome is that he meets his future wife, a pretty and intelligent student, at his next school. She falls, strangely enough I think, for his eyes. All his students think highly of him at his new school as well.

10 Life after Zhang Yu, 1950 - 1952

The Shanghai Dressmaking Co was never the same after PaPa's sudden death. The energy and vitality was gone and an emptiness lingered in the air. It did not take long before some customers moved on. Some old faithfuls, English and Chinese customers, continued to come. Zhang Yu's cousin and assistant, Cheong, continued as manager, but he did not have Yu's ability or initiative. His heart was not in the business and he was not given any incentive. It was merely a job. MahMah made all the decisions, and there was no way he would be handed the business. He could not keep the shifus in line. They did not respect him like they did Yu. One by one the shifus left to start their own dress-making businesses. However the Shanghai Dressmaking Co went on for some years.

The dressmaking shop needed Yu's personal touch, but OIC was different. The dry cleaning shop was still doing well, as it was a favourite with the British. The workers were all still there and business hummed along as before. Profits were still coming in, the workers received good wages, and the kitchen continued to supply quality meals.

When Christmas came around there was still need for overtime. Three hours each evening in the week before Christmas. The lights were all on and the atmosphere was festive. Little Li was at OIC, a bit more subdued, for she was growing up. When PaPa was alive she was always skipping around the two shops. In those days both shops had been lit up before Christmas, as both did overtime. Each evening had ended with a big supper. It was a lively season. The workers received their bonuses and enjoyed a big feed each night. Now with Zhang Yu gone only OIC was lit up. The Shanghai Dressmaking Co was in darkness.

*

The caning inflicted by MahMah on Yeh and Li slowed down and came to a halt in 1951. School activities filled the lives of the Zhang siblings. Yeh and Li turned their attention to sport.

They both found they enjoyed running and that it was something they did well.

*

With Zhang Yu's death and Ah Chieh leaving the family, life became lonely and empty for MahMah. She was no longer the senior wife of a prosperous businessman, respected, envied and feared. The good income from the dressmaking business had gone, like her husband. Slowly her habits also changed. By 1952 she stopped inviting friends home to smoke opium. She had always slept late, but now she was up and out before noon to the illegal opium dens in Chinatown. Why? Was it because of the raid by the police?

One evening sister Meng and I had been absolutely terrified when a British police officer leading two local policemen burst into our shophouse. Being English educated we were able to learn from the officer that it was an opium raid. It was all over within an hour. Strangely, they checked the sitting room and the kitchen but did not go into the bedrooms. In the master bedroom were the opium pipes and all the opium paraphernalia. Sister Meng instructed me to help her hide the opium pipes amongst the kindling (and the horrid cockroaches!) in the kitchen after the police left. She was afraid they would come back. When MahMah returned later we related the incident to her. She had little to say to us. Later, Meng told me that it was not a "true" raid, for the police had been bribed!

From then on MahMah frequented the illegal opium den in Petaling Street in Chinatown. I remember the first occasion I went to the den. While OIC still earned good profits we kept the green coloured Morris Minor and our old driver Yusoff. It was late afternoon. I had sports practice and Yusoff picked me up from school. Instead of going home he drove into the city, taking me to Chinatown. He pointed to a small shop, telling me to go in and get MahMah. I entered a heavily curtained dark room. Of course I could smell the opium.

Some four persons were lying on a large raised wooden platform. There were two opium lamps with the usual opium paraphernalia and two people on each side of the lamp. I made out MahMah's shape, the only female amongst them. She was just lying there, so she must have finished her smoke. There was an emaciated looking man puffing away on an opium pipe. Little Li's appearance was ignored. She was no disturbance. They were deep in their opium dreams!

11 Teenage Life

The world of boys, 1954-1957

It is 1954 and I am not interested in boys yet. My sisters talk about a very pretty and rich girl from our school who is some four years older than me. She has a crush on this tall, good looking boy called Kit. My sisters are invited to her birthday party. At the party Kit invites Mei to dance, which upsets the birthday girl and she cries.

However, I get to know some boys. I go along to the movies. I get noticed and taken on some outings. Tagging along with sister Mei, I meet Xin, who is a classmate of her boyfriend and Kit's as well. I do not even know whether I like Xin, but his attention is welcome; besides, it is cool to have a boyfriend in senior school. Xin lives nearby and visits me at the shop. He does not get a good reception. My father growls at him, my brother Sang calls him Tomato face. It does not take long for me to lose interest, so I tell him to please not visit me anymore.

Then I meet someone more interesting and better looking! Teck is a swimmer, tall, tanned and broad-shouldered. He becomes my new boyfriend. I see him occasionally and we hold hands.

A couple of months later I meet another boy, Hua, who is most persistent in pursuing me. Teck's sister is my good friend and she tells her brother to knock it off, as Hua is determined to win me as his girlfriend.

Hua is tenacious. He has his own car, is doing an apprenticeship and expects to go to study in England. He is an accomplished dancer and does the quick waltz, my favourite dance, better than anyone else. He takes me to the movies and buys me bags of candy. At the roadside hawkers' stalls we dine on a variety of dishes. He spends on me and has no trouble with funds. Hua is not a great looker, but he does have something special: the gift of laughter. He makes me laugh. He teases me unceasingly and flatters me, always telling me I have beautiful eyes.

Kuala Lumpur is a magical place where life is so peaceful in the 1950s. There is one special evening when the moon and stars are out, and although it is only a little after ten o'clock, it is peaceful and quiet. Hua takes me to Stadium Merdeka and pushes me on the big swings there. I am laughing with glee as I go higher and higher on the swing. Hua becomes my first love.

It is an innocent boy-girl romance. Hua is smart and shrewd but respects me, and we keep our relationship virtuous. He asks me to wait for him, and even if I am going with another guy when he returns in three years' time I must promise to see him. He tells me I must stay single and give him a chance to win me back. For the next two months he tries to brainwash me. I must promise to see him again when he returns! Soon he leaves and I feel lonely. I had one person who cared for me, and now he is gone. Hua writes to me every week. I go through 1956 missing Hua and I have no interest in other boys or parties.

1957 finds me bright and energetic again. I enjoy my prefect's duties and laksa lunch at school. One day I get a phone call from Kit. He asks me to date his classmate and good friend Jin. They are on holidays, as it is university vacation time. Kit has a new girlfriend, but that is his business. Jin turns out to be very good at jiving, which is the latest rage in town. I love dancing, so I go out with Jin again. I allow him to hold my hand, but I am not into him. Jin turns up next vacation, but I refuse to go out with him as I am honestly not interested.

*

There is good news in school. I am told to go to the office, as Miss Carpenter wishes to see me. Miss Carpenter was our headmistress. She was fond of the Zhang sisters. We would speak up in English while the other girls would run away. She attended my church wedding service when she learnt of it, although I had not sent out any invitations. We corresponded for a while when she retired to England.

Form Five farewell with teachers and classmates, 1957. Li is indicated by the arrow

Back to the school office. Both I and the other girl who sat the entrance exam for Sixth Form have been accepted. Miss Carpenter is pleased. I have the better result. She congratulates me, but also offers me the only teacher trainee position for next year. She had offered sister Mei the same the year before. She tells me that if I work steadily I should get a grade one, just as Mei did. However, she advises me to do sixth form, as she wants me to go on to tertiary education. At home, my mother pressures me to take shorthand and typing classes. She has no ambitions for me. She points to sister Meng's example. Meng is doing well at office work. Meng is dutiful. She hands our mother half her salary each month!

Time passes, and my Senior Cambridge Examinations are about to begin. Two events stand out. The first has to do with my father.

It is early afternoon and there is a heavy downpour. I am desperately running around, dressed in my school prefect uniform, trying to get a taxi to school, where the exams are held. I see my father seated inside the shop watching me. The year before when Mei sat for the exams he sent her in his car.

This year he knows what is happening but makes no attempt to help me.

I organise my own transport. The exams are vital for my future. I no longer expect love, but I still cannot understand how he can wish me ill, for I am still his daughter. I get to school and sit for the first paper. I survive.

The second event, two days later, is almost a disaster. Like my father, I take a short afternoon nap. I wake and check my exam schedule. I have made a mistake. Today's paper starts at 4.15 pm, not 5.15 pm. I get to school in a taxi and find my classmates are all seated inside the school hall answering the exam questions.

I control the trembling and panic within me and force myself to walk calmly into the hall towards the chief invigilator seated at the desk in front of all the students. All eyes turn to look at me in shock and pity. The others have been at their desks for more than half an hour. I put on my sweetest smile and stroll past as if I do not have a care in the world! The chief invigilator walks towards me. "You had an accident?" I cannot speak, just nod in reply.

Bless the kind soul. She leads me to the only unoccupied desk in the hall and hands me a question paper. I take 10 minutes to compose myself. An hour passes. I am scribbling desperately, as I know I am very short of time. Soon the students get up and leave the hall. The invigilator is kind and gives me another half an hour, so I have only lost forty minutes. I have been very lucky, as I still manage to get a credit. But this is the easiest subject of the examinations.

The rest of the exams do not go well for me. I self-destruct! I could not have wished for a better English Literature paper but leave my favourite question to answer last. My exam technique is poor. I am a slow writer and have spent too much time on the earlier questions. Only two sentences into my last question the announcement is made: "Time is up, stop writing!" One distinction gone!

A few days later I self-destruct again with my religious knowledge paper. I have answered one question less. Another easy distinction gone. For my third favourite subject, history, I run short of study time. I took the wrong punt, choosing the wrong topics and administrators for the British History of India. Another hoped-for distinction gone! I do not need to wait until January for my results, knowing I have not done well.

*

The year 1957 is special for the country. August 31st is Independence Day, marking Malaya's break from Britain. The year before sister Mei and I had the honour of meeting the chief minister, Tengku Abdul Rahman. He was taking a walk near the famous Lake Gardens. We saw him, dashed across the road, shook his hand and ran off. Through the mists of time I recall a very warm and kind smile. I do not recall there being any bodyguards.

Miss Carpenter gave us a very special lesson on what independence means. Specific privileges for the Malays are absolutely imperative. They are a very gentle race who must be assisted. The British felt a moral obligation to leave political power to the Malays. The more aggressive Chinese already held the economic power. But there was another problem. The Malaysian Communist Party was largely Chinese, and their loyalties were suspect. New, stronger and more vocal Malay leaders like Tun Abdul Razak had appeared on the political horizon.

It is a peaceful transition of power in August 1957. Life is unchanged and mine continues unruffled. It is near Christmas when I am invited by a friend to be her brother's partner at a dance. Out steps the most gorgeous guy I have ever set eyes on. I had seen him as a young boy in church. Now he is six foot tall with compelling deep set eyes! His features are western, as he has European blood. I have a new boyfriend!

*

It is now 1958, and life in a co-education class is different and so interesting after eleven years in a girls' school. The Indian boys in my class are short in stature, but they are so smart. There are many male teachers, and they are well dressed. I am active in school, involved in mock elections and a school play. My gorgeous boyfriend and I do not meet often but we write to each other, as he is in college in another Malayan state.

Li, aged 17

Meanwhile, I still correspond with Hua, who has not yet returned from England.

I am flattered by my new boyfriend. He has a photograph of me on his desk, and tells me in a letter that a mate of his has seen the same picture in the largest photo shop in Kuala Lumpur. New boyfriend proudly tells his mate that the girl is his new girlfriend. A second photo of me is displayed in another shop. Big eyes and long Chinese hair do look good in photos. It helps to be photogenic!

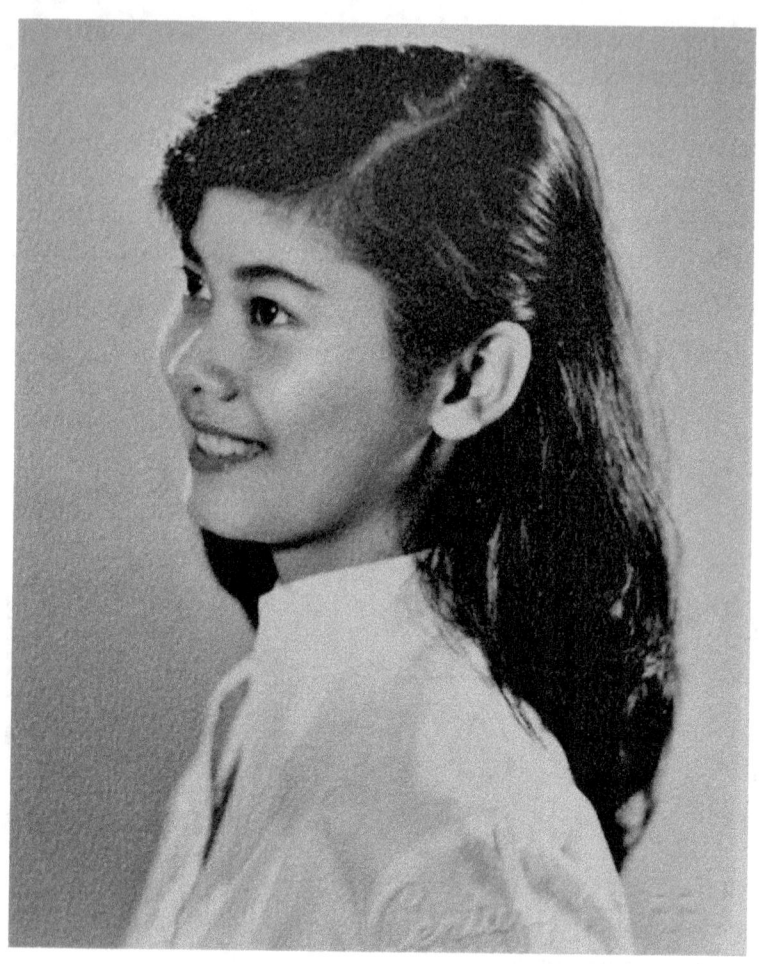

The displayed photo of Li, aged 17

Out of the blue Kit appears. Soon we are dating.

What happened to my gorgeous Eurasian boyfriend? In a moment of lucidity, I realised there was no future for him and me. Traditionally, a husband should be older, and we are the same age. I will be in terrible trouble with my father. He would never allow me to marry, let alone have a steady boyfriend, who is not Chinese. I hardly know him. Better to break up early than when I get too attached! I write to say that I will not be seeing him anymore.

Kit storms into my world. I am seventeen in sixth form, he is twenty in second year medicine. He is dashing and appears on his big motorbike. Tall, well-built and good looking. How can my teenage classmates and friends compare? Yes, Kit, you blew everyone out of the water. Yes, my father, the pair of bright eyes that you would have preferred to give to Mei seem to have worked on Kit too!

I am impressed by Kit, but it is definitely not a case of love at first sight, and I thought of him as my sister's vintage. Our paths had crossed a number of times, first in 1955 when I was dating Hua. We had gone on a group picnic at Port Dickson, a nearby seaside resort. A couple slightly older than us asked for a lift back to Kuala Lumpur. It was Kit and his girlfriend.

Another day, Mei and I were watching a parade passing our shop. Mei recognised the sergeant major leading a detachment of cadet corps from a top Kuala Lumpur school. It was Kit.

Mei took me on an excursion organised by her boyfriend to see the wildlife at Templer Park. Included was Kit and his girlfriend. Years later he says that he remembers me as the girl with the dark eyes and the fat calves. I was wearing shorts. I am the only one of the four Zhang girls with big leg muscles! Kit also tells me that his classmate, Xin, would brag to him about visiting this new girl (me) who lived near him. Maybe that kept me at the back of Kit's mind!

The happy student years, 1958-1959

The two years in Sixth Form are my happiest at school. I am with a bunch of lively classmates. There are always jokes and laughter. I enjoy friendships with the girls. Attractive Anna with her slightly crooked smile. She is the class sexpot. Then there is Fugie the tomboy. Some girls do not like her because she loves to use long English words that she herself does not understand. But I get along with her. When her brother leaves for England she takes over his scooter and I am her favourite passenger. Who knows, I might have gone out with the tall basketball player after all had Kit not turned up!

Sixth Form girls at the Victorian Institution in 1958. Li is third from the left in the middle row

Back on vacation, Kit visits me in the afternoon as I stay late at school for compulsory library sessions. He used to be school captain here. He comes on his big motorbike. I am told that in Singapore he roars through the campus with his two friends. They call themselves The Brothers Karamazov!

His classmate Irene tells me he is popular with the girls. He is playful and neglects his studies. He cuts lectures, but gets found out because his name appears three times on the attendance list. Kind friends have signed for him!

Kit receives a shock when his name is not on the list of students who have passed. He is better known by the lecturers for the noise he makes on his motorbike than as a serious student. He rides back to Kuala Lumpur and there is an unhappy meeting with his parents. He is an only son and has deeply disappointed the parents he cherishes. They will "lose face" with relatives and friends.

They want to know why he failed. They do not think his brains are lacking, so it must be playfulness and distraction. What about his new girlfriend? His father asks him to give her up. He refuses. He promises to study but will not give up his girlfriend. Years later his father tells me this, trying to strengthen the bonds between Kit and me while his mother tries to split us up.

Before long Kit takes me home to meet his parents. His father looks fearsome, but I am to find that he is one of the most wonderful people in this world. His mother prattles on. She is quick to let me know that Kit is a prize catch! She giggles as she deliberately lets out that he may be a bit of a playboy and is likely to play the field rather than stick to one girl! I am most amused. I would like to play the field too. I still have a boyfriend abroad and am not serious about Kit. It is Kit who reminds me that the first day of March is special since he first took me out on that day.

I am invited to the house again, even while Kit is away on campus. On one such occasion, when his mother Grace is alone with me, she tells me that she has no control over Kit's taste for girls, nor over how long his interest in me will last. They knew the parents of his previous girlfriend and it was embarrassing to them when Kit broke up with her. She obviously does not expect us to last as a couple. I laugh within myself. I am not sure I want to stick with your son!

*

It is the latter half of 1959. I am in Upper Sixth Form and still with Kit. I have good results from the lower sixth results. I get lazy, skip classes and pretend to be sick, hiding in the girls' room.

Kit's father, KM, learns that I do not have a desk, lamp or room of my own at the shophouse. He invites me to move in with him and Grace. Except for vacation, when Kit comes home, there is no one else there. I move into the guest room. There is good food, peace, quiet and outings to the movies, but I am not doing well with my studies. I am still lazy and easily distracted. We have a new literature lecturer and the lessons become even more boring! Kit comes back for a short break and I am happy. I only allow him to hug me and hold my hand.

The Higher School Certificate examination finally arrives. I am stupid again. Kit has given me his Parker 51 fountain pen for luck. I am not used to it, besides which I am still a slow writer. I am also sentimental and will not give up the pen. Again, I do not finish my papers.

There is an excursion to Bangkok, organised by the Thai ambassador's son, a student at our school. Some of my classmates have signed up and I am not going to miss out! It is a ten-day train journey to Thailand. The trip is well organised and cheap. There is a big group of us from school, including several teachers. It is my first time outside Malaya and I find it so exciting.

A favourite teacher, Mr A, talks about taking me to the Imperial Hotel in Bangkok to watch the sunset. I hear that the famous author Somerset Maugham wrote *The Painted Veil* when he stayed there. It is said to be a beautiful hotel with fabulous sunset views. Mr A is popular with the female classmates. He is not particularly handsome, but he does have blue eyes and long eyelashes! I get along with him and we chat when we meet at some of the sightseeing tours. Thailand is beautiful and so exotic. The scenes are stunning and the company so lively, I cannot but enjoy this trip.

The sunset trip does not take place. I think the two lady teachers, who are also kind and friendly to me, have warned Mr A not to start a teacher-student romance. I am still naïve, thinking we could be friends. I already have a boyfriend and Mr A knows it. I return to Kuala Lumpur with the group. I lose my voice from too much singing with the crowd. Kit is amused when he hears me sing the latest hit tune Waterloo in a cracked voice.

*

My school life was very enjoyable. Then life moves on. Sister Mei returns from two years of teacher training in England. Kit's father is keen to know my family. He goes to the airport to meet Mei, who is her charming self. She speaks good English and impresses Kit's parents.

My mother is also there at the meeting. She is gushing in her report to my father. She tells him in Shanghainese that Mei is a "knockout" with Kit's parents, not realising that I understand the dialect, although I do not speak it. She sighs and says it would be nice if Kit were Mei's boyfriend and wishes it were so. Besides, he would be a doctor. Oh my mother! Of course, both you and my father want the best for your favourites.

I am deeply hurt by my parents, and relay the incident to Kit. He is annoyed with his parents for some reason. He blurts out "I have no feelings for and am not interested in Mei. My girlfriend is my own business! I decide who I want for a girlfriend and future partner. It is my right, and the decision does not rest with my parents." I am consoled. A year before he had asked me if I had ever thought of becoming his life partner. I was surprised, for I had not thought that far!

In early 1960, Kit's mother gets me a temporary job at the Chinese school where she teaches English. My treatment at the school is good and I am well paid.

Portrait of KM, my father-in-law

KM was a most unusual person. I have not met anyone else like him in my life. He was the father I never had and I loved him. Physically, he was larger than the average Chinese male. He was better muscled than my father, as he did weights and had been an athlete, participating in shot put events in the National Games of China, a competition for expatriates, in Shanghai during 1935. He also did high jump and sprint events, but was best at the shot put. Kit inherited his size, height and fair complexion. But what drew me to KM was his beautiful smile. Kit inherited that smile. When I met KM he was in his forties, overweight, and carried a stern look. I thought my father was better looking, but KM had so much more: intelligence, foresight and nuanced understanding of others, but most of all he had so much love to give.

KM came from a large family, but his father died when he was still young, and he was harshly disciplined by an older brother. His father had come to Kuala Lumpur from southern China as an 18 year old migrant, strongly built, offering his services as a labourer. He had married a nonya, a descendent of Chinese immigrants whose family had been in Malaya for some generations.

KM's father had done well. He died fairly young, however he left his large family well provided for. When KM was 18 his teacher, a Catholic priest, advised his older brother that KM was intelligent and should be sent to England to do law, as his abilities seem to lie in that direction. However, by that time the family's fortunes had declined. Apparently the mother and other older offspring were gamblers and had been cheated of much of their wealth. There was no money left for KM to study abroad. Grace often mentioned that she tried to encourage KM to do law in the UK. She was certain she could manage with her two children, as she enjoyed a good salary. Others had gone and been successful. Her good friend Felicity and husband had been one such case. But KM refused.

KM did plan meticulously for his children. The children learnt English from KM and Grace, as they were both English educated and had passed the senior Cambridge exams. The children spoke and wrote good English. They were well disciplined. They had study time and play time. They were taught good manners, but more importantly, good principles to live by.

In comparison, my father spent little time with his children. In the Zhang family, the elders did the thinking. But PaPa was often occupied with his business problems or with those of the Shanghainese community. MahMah was in charge of the children, but spent little time on them. Her philosophy at the time was "the children will grow anyway, just feed them." And it never occurred to Jen that he needed to plan for his children. He had been taught to follow, and he did his job faithfully.

I knew KM for 6 years, but he was bigger than life to me. Kit loved him but also feared him. So did Grace. Behind that stern exterior was so much compassion and love. He loved his siblings and his nephews and all who sought his help. He was always trying to help others.

Little Li had been like him. She also had so much love to give, although, throughout her childhood, no one wanted it! Love does not have to be confined to blood relations. KM was never afraid to speak his mind and play the villain. I believe that was something that linked us. I was not afraid to play the villain, having been the scapegoat for so much of my young life. I believe KM had an insight into people. I felt that he could see Grace's weaknesses, but loved her deeply.

I saw a different side of Grace, but since she showed me no love and inflicted so much pain on me I did not make concessions for her. KM controlled her. I believe he protected me. If he had not liked me then Grace would have gotten rid of me long before. She seemed to sincerely believe I was a threat and not good enough for her son. She was protective of Kit and wanted the best for him!

KM agreed to her son's marriage, not Grace.

Yes, KM, we enjoyed a certain companionship. I could chat and laugh with you, but never with Grace. You knew something of my love-hate relationship with Jen. I think you knew I would have loved to have a father like you. And although I had no accomplishments, wealth or academic prowess, you were proud of me. I remember the occasion in 1958 when you took a whole lot of photos to your cousin's shop for developing. Your cousin's wife thought you had taken photos of the Hong Kong actress Lin Dai, because my eyes looked so like hers. Others had mentioned the resemblance to me before. You proudly told her that the girl in the photograph was your future daughter-in-law!

Hong Kong actress Lin Dai in 1957

Li in 1958

You also told me that, when Kit's exam results were not as expected, you and Grace had asked him to give up his new girlfriend, who must have been the distraction. You told me that Kit promised to study hard, but refused to give up the new girlfriend!

I remembered the occasion you spoke up for Kit. I told you in January 1960 that I was going out with my old boyfriend Hua and that I had told Kit about it. I had promised Hua five years before that I would go out with him when he returned from his studies abroad. I promised to give us a chance to find out how we felt about each other. You were afraid I might choose Hua. You told me I was being grossly unfair, as Kit was in Singapore and not on the spot. While KM tried hard to strengthen the bonds between Kit and me, Grace did not want us together. I wonder why Grace did not take the opportunity to get rid of me then!

*

My life took a different direction when I agreed to date Kit. I was young and inexperienced, succumbing to the comfortable life KM provided when I moved into their home. I recall one clash in the 1980s, provoked by Grace, when I told Kit he had intruded into my world in 1958. I had been a happy 17 year old, enjoying sixth form life and the company of my classmates, males and females. He was not part of my life, I had no interest in him, why did he decide to pursue me? My future was irrevocably changed to one I would not have chosen had I known the consequences of being won over by Kit.

I could not come to you, KM, to tell you what Grace was doing to me. In the Zhang family we also had our values. I realised that you owed me nothing, but owed Grace much. She was your wife, mother of your two beloved children. Her income from teaching provided the luxuries to the family. I gave you nothing of substance.

In your last letter, which arrived after you departed this life, you spoke of your love for me and your pain that I had not been coming to you for our chit chats. I was in pain too, for I could not explain things to you. I think I am flawed. I am over-sensitive. I am not able to brush aside criticism. I am not able to pretend and flatter. I am an abysmal failure at pandering to Grace. Your death was sudden. How do you measure grief? I know your family's grief is deep but I, too, grieve for you. I am not related by blood, but if you prick me I bleed just as much!

My father in law, I can never forget your beautiful smile, which I believe comes from the soul. It is only because of you that I went to university, something I hadn't dreamed of. Although it might have been better to let me find my own way, carve my own path as a secretary in the commercial world. It would have avoided the antagonism I suffered from your wife and daughter.

You were an overly stern father to your son because you believed you detected a weakness in him that was not in your daughter. To you, Kit was playful, keen to experience the world, but not tough enough to handle life's trials. You wanted him to have your strength. He did learn from you. He learned to have a deep attachment to his parents. When you left, it was all transferred to his mother. But, KM, how much can one prepare for the future when life is unpredictable!

Grace, my mother-in-law

When Kit passed away I lost interest in this earthly life. I wanted to give Grace the benefit of the doubt and blame myself for all my problems. If Kit could love his mother so much surely she cannot have caused so much hurt to others. In writing my book I have reopened my wounds, my pain resurfaces and thoughts crowd my mind.

It is January 2022 as I write these words. It was in 1960, 62 years ago, that Grace started her mind games on me. I had not wanted to dwell on it, but it is the core of my pain and hurt. It seems to hit me where I am most vulnerable. So many years ago, but it does feel like yesterday, because I am raw and bleeding again.

*

Felicity was Grace's best friend at that time, and she chose to hurt me, although I had not offended her. She was a self-declared clairvoyant, as well as claiming to be close to God. She and Grace inflicted so much pain on me. Perhaps it was fun and games for them.

How did it start? Felicity was the one to give Grace her Christian name. They were on the ladies' church committee together. Grace had introduced me as her son's girlfriend. I know that Felicity liked Kit and had a young daughter. She possibly had her own plans and designs. It did not bother me because I felt that we lived in a modern time when parents do not matchmake anymore and we choose our own partners. But Felicity was a shrewd person and could read Grace. She found that Grace enjoyed hearing uncomplimentary things about me and became bold. My physiognomy according to Felicity:

- Forehead: too small, lacking in intelligence
- Mouth: too weak, lacking in direction
- Chin: too small, lacking in character
- Cheeks: not high enough to look good
- Eyes: too dark, could harbour bad intentions or rebellion.

Grace added that there was fire in my eyes, indicating boldness, compared to the gentleness in her own. Overall, not a good face, with no hint of bringing prosperity to a future husband's family. The most damning thing was that my face had no sign of Fook (luck or grace) to bring to the Lee family household. This was brought up again when Grace attacked me verbally after returning to the house following the funeral of Kit's father. She said I should have never been allowed to marry into the Lee family.

There was an occasion that Grace took great delight in relating to me. Felicity was serving tea to the committee ladies when Grace announced that her son was getting engaged. Grace said Felicity was so affected that her hand trembled, making the cup rattle, spilling tea onto the saucer. Grace made it a point to let me know that Felicity did not like me, but that poor Felicity had no choice; she merely read what was written on my face. However, Grace professed to be open-minded and said she did not allow her best friend to influence her, besides which, I was her son's choice, not hers.

I told Kit about Felicity. Kit said Felicity was a stupid woman and not to waste time thinking about her. Perhaps I should have taken it up with Kit's father. Meanwhile, I started to realise that Kit was too conflict-averse to say anything to Grace about how I was being treated.

*

In early 1960 Kit's sister Chun gave a tea and cakes reception at her home for the wedding of their cousin Mimi. I had originally been approached to be Mimi's bridesmaid. A few weeks later the request was withdrawn. Her young cousin of some 14 years wanted it badly so she was to have it. Kit was the best man.

I was in a happy mood. I was also in a new cheongsam and it was a pretty one. All the relatives were there. Grace beckoned to a happy, laughing Li. Just before university started I had become engaged to Kit. Grace had told me I was the luckiest girl around, as Kit was such a prized catch. Yes, I considered myself lucky. But we had been going steady for two years.

We were alone at the far corner of the garden, away from everyone else. "Li, can you stay away from the photos? I do not want you in a single one. We are all related by blood. You are not a relative." Tears came to my eyes. I was a relative to be. Grace walked away.

When Kit and I went back to the university hostel I was crying and clumsily told him what Grace had said to me. All I got was a ticking off. His mother was a kindly person not capable of being mean or spiteful.

My sense of decency did not allow me to tell KM or Chun what had occurred. In hindsight, I can see that it was a crucial time, time for me to leave that household, but Li did not have the foresight, experience or strength.

Li did not realise it at the time, but Grace had shown her true colours.

*

Grace still sees me as a passing fancy for Kit, even though we are engaged to be married.

On one occasion, I am tanned from a trip to the seaside with Kit. Grace avoids the sun, as she considers fairness a beauty feature. She muses that a Shanghainese girl should be pale with a good complexion. She notes that I am short sighted, although I do have a pair of bright eyes and a petite figure. (She is short sighted herself). Grace also notices that, while I am not busty, I am not flat-chested as a lot of Chinese girls are. She laments that her daughter did not inherit her full figure and that Chinese men fail to appreciate full figures.

*

Two years have gone by, and I am not the passing fancy that Grace hoped for. However, she points out that I bring nothing to their family. She herself had come from a family of modest means, yet I am subjected to this scrutiny. I have no dowry. My father is not the sole owner, only part-owner, of a dry cleaning business. Besides, there are so many children in the family. Moreover, I come from a community that is not highly rated by her.

Grace again notes that I have no special talents, play no musical instrument, have no minor skills such as sewing or embroidery, although my family owns the biggest dressmaking shop in Kuala Lumpur. Kit knows that I am my honest self. I do not boast of anything.

Grace never states what she wants or declares her intentions. She will not allow herself to be seen as anything other than kind and supportive. I wish she had openly told me to get lost, but I think she was afraid of offending Kit. I would have gone. Instead, she waits and hopes that he will drop me. But something does happen. KM starts to plan a university education for me. Grace never dares oppose her husband.

I had no ambitions for tertiary education, as I knew there would be no support from my father. I had gone into sixth form and matriculated only to improve my chances of getting a better job than I would have done otherwise.

By this stage Grace seems to have realised she will have great difficulty controlling me. A ray of light appears when I tell her Kit and I are thinking of splitting up. She swiftly informs Kit's father. KM quickly informs me that his offer to finance my studies still stands. Kit rushes home to tell me that he does not want to break up, that he does not want to give me up. I know I am vulnerable. I have learned to appreciate Kit's noble nature, his kindness and gentleness. It will be hard to find someone like him. He is earnest, he asks me not to leave him. With him before me his mother's image fades into the background.

I know that Grace wants to be rid of me. I know that KM wants me to stay with Kit. I give in to Kit.

Sister-in-law Chun

I had heard so much about Chun. Only good. I was frightened to meet her. The first time took place in 1960 when she returned to Kuala Lumpur after two years in Australia. Kit warned me that she and her husband were very serious people and not given to socialising, besides being very religious. I found her cool, polite and distant. Her eyes were searching, but it was okay as I had done nothing wrong and had nothing to hide. I behaved normally. I did not know how much her father had told her about me. I did not try to get on Chun's good side and just kept quiet.

How mistaken I was! Twenty years later Chun let out that she had been suspicious of me. I was the gold digger. She said straight to my face that I had caused her two years of misery in Australia, although she had since forgiven me.

Chun had been expecting a child during their time in Australia and they were short of funds. She planned to borrow money from her parents, as half her husband's salary went to pay his two brothers' tertiary education fees. She had no doubt that her parents would help, just as they had financed her university education. Kit had won a state scholarship for his medical studies. He had told me that, since his parents did not pay his fees, he thought it was okay if they paid my three years of tertiary education. He never mentioned this opinion to his sister.

Chun therefore did not expect to hear from her father that he and Grace had decided to finance a degree for her brother's girlfriend. That extra cash to which she felt entitled was gone and there was no point in asking for it. Who to blame but the outsider Li?

The idea of university had never even entered my mind, but Kit's father was always big hearted and wanted to help me improve myself. When Grace found that her son was not likely to dump me, she felt that a daughter-in-law with a degree would certainly look better.

Sister-in-law Chun, I did you no wrong. I understood that you were a close knit family and not keen on outsiders. But I could not resist your father's offer.

That your father preferred my sons is again not my fault. I knew your deep love for each other, but you were more concerned with your husband. You could have done more to include your father in your family's life!

I think you tried to be fair, but in the end sided with your mother. Your constant reminding that I took "her" money was a source of hurt, while it confirmed Grace's feeling that she had a right to dominate me.

Ten years after I got my arts degree we managed to save the money and I returned to Grace the M$7,000 she and KM had paid out for my studies. You did not believe me because Grace never told you about it and you said that she told you everything. You did not know your mother, so the outsider must be a liar!

I was always respectful to you, Chun. Even when I differed in my thinking I never argued with you. I sat through your lectures. You told me off when my son was pursuing pretty girls and I took it silently.

But I know that your two sons, one autistic, the other with an intellectual disability, gave you much to cope with, something your husband did not manage. He lived in a world of his own, unwilling to accept the reality that his sons could never live independent, successful lives.

Chun needed help herself and ultimately turned a blind eye to Li's one big problem. That is life.

12 Marriage

The 1960s

In 1960 and 1961 I am at university in Singapore and go back to Kuala Lumpur only during vacation. A truce is on with Grace. I have as few conversations as possible with her, but I hurt KM, who enjoys chit chats with me.

In early 1962 Kit and I get married. KM is very happy, although worried, as neither of us have graduated yet. An unexpected pregnancy happens. KM and Grace are even more worried. Kit stands firm, no abortion. Grace pulls me aside and offers me two bottles of castor oil. She tells me she has aborted in the past with only a mild stomach ache. She tells me I have to do it, because the disruption of the baby could mean the end of a medical future for Kit. She stresses that I must make sacrifices, that I am young enough to have many more babies later on. This is to be our secret. I swallow the castor oil and spend hours on the toilet feeling that my guts will all spill out. But the baby does not.

It is a strong pregnancy and our son arrives at the end of the year. I take him back to Kit's parents in Kuala Lumpur and return to Singapore for my final examination. Kit sits for his finals two months later. 1963 rolls in and we have both passed our exams. There is less time with Grace, and she is content as there is the grandson to play with. KM derives great joy from the baby. He dotes on the child.

Come early 1964 and Kit is sent on a rural posting. In March I have a second boy. KM asks Kit for the older child, to bring him up in Kuala Lumpur. Kit knows splitting up the boys would upset me. He knows that the company of my siblings gave me the only pleasure I had in my lonely childhood and refuses his father's request. His father accepts it as the right thing to do. His mother is hurt.

The house where we lived during Kit's rural posting

*

Then a tragic episode. KM collapses from a heart attack. It is fatal. We return to the house after the funeral, all having one of the saddest days in our lives. I have my own private grief. Grace, Chun and her husband, Kit and I are all on the cushioned rattan seats in the sitting room. Grace turns to me and empties out her hostility. "You are the most ungrateful person. You owe Dad so much, how do you expect to be forgiven? What did you do to make him happy? Have you done anything for him?" She continues "I should never have allowed you to be married into this household. Felicity warned me about you long ago, but I was too kind."

Chun interrupts Grace "Why are you saying such harsh words to Li?"

Kit is quiet, shut up in a world of pain, for he loved his father deeply. Even if he heard her he would never blame his mother because of her grief. Kit would not accept that his mother could be spiteful. I slip out of the house and drive away in his Volvo. The attempt at suicide starts.

I drive to a mining pond some eight or nine kilometres away. I sit in the car at the edge of the vast pond, crying and gathering the courage to drive in. Do I pander to Grace by removing myself? I know she hates me. I have known for six years. My relationship with Kit's father was so different. He was so warm.

Now here I am at the edge of the mining pond. All I have to do is press down on the accelerator and shoot in. I am 24, married for two years, with 18 month and three month old sons. A husband who is kind and gentle.

I have so much to live for. Do I owe Grace so much? Only my disappearance will please her. I know she will never accept any blame. She will be only too glad to say that I am mentally unbalanced! Kit is still young and will marry again. There is a good chance that his next wife will be more acceptable to Grace. I think and try to work up courage for an hour. I can only weep as I think of my sons, especially the youngest. I cannot do it. With a sense of failure and cowardice I drive home.

Nobody even noticed I had been missing.

*

After going back in time to write my book, I am able to see certain truths and can answer Grace's question: have you done anything for him? Grace allowed her hostility to cloud her memory. Yes, I did do something for KM, although I was not given credit for it.

While Kit and I stayed in the one-room hospital quarters while he did compulsory houseman's training before being allowed to go out to work, my first baby, with his amah, stayed at my in-laws. For over a year KM was a very happy and contented grandfather. I know that Grace also loved her grandson. KM watched the baby grow, was delighted with the greedy boy's appetite, insisting on increasing his milk consumption above the recommended amount. The child became grossly overweight. KM wanted a big boy. At the time

KM passed away he was waiting for the boy to talk and call him Grandpa. Unfortunately, my son did not start to talk until two months after KM went.

By allowing my son to live with him and Grace, KM experienced the joy of being a grandfather. It is truly a wonderful feeling, I know, for I enjoy being a grandmother.

From KM's final letter to me, I also know for sure that I brought him enjoyment from our conversations together.

Yes, Grace, I did do things that made KM happy. I did do things for him.

*

My last meaningful encounter with Grace is in 1973. After this I lose all respect for her. It is May. Kit has met somebody else and my marriage may be at its end. I had not suspected any third person, for although Kit has been somewhat remote, we have not quarrelled. There have been no unkind words. Life seemed normal. It turns out that divorce was never on Kit's mind, he just wants his fun, to have a mistress. But I will not put up with it! For me it is all or nothing.

I tell myself that my dignity is not important, but my family is. I make myself beg Grace for help. I know my father-in-law would help me without fail, but he is gone, and Grace has always claimed great influence over her son.

I tell Grace that my marriage is in trouble. Could she talk to Kit and remind him that he has a family. The children are eleven, nine, seven and I am heavily pregnant with number four.

"No, I will not speak to my son. This is a private matter between the two of you."

I swallow my pride, asking again on behalf of the children – her grandchildren.

"No, he is a grown man. He knows what he is doing. This is your private business and has nothing to do with me." She adds for good measure "Now you know the difference between a wife and a mother. You can divorce a wife but not your mother. A mother is forever, a wife is only good as long as she is able to hold her husband's sexual interest."

Bluntly I say I will not live in the same town if my husband has a mistress installed. I will seek a divorce. Grace clearly finds this acceptable. She inquires, since I have stated I will never stand for a second establishment á la Ipoh style, when will I leave? Obviously, I cannot go while I am waddling like a duck. I have to be fit. But I still believe in myself and that I have a life ahead of me. I will join my brother Yeh in Australia after I give birth.

But by the time my fourth child, a third son, is born in Ipoh, Kit's affair has come to an end and my resolve to leave diminishes. Life and our marriage return to a sort of normalcy, although I retain a sense of insecurity for the remainder of my life.

The last word about Grace

Grace remained a source of friction between me and Kit. Every meeting with her ended in a period of coolness between us. Grace continued to play the victim, while I was once again cast in the role of villain, coming to believe it as I suffered my undiagnosed depression.

In 1999, after her second partner, San, had died, Grace hinted that she was thinking of emigrating to Australia, moving in with us. Chun gave me the tip-off, so in my tactless way, I confronted Kit. If she moves in, I will leave.

"She has never given up trying to destroy my marriage."

"Can't she come over for a visit?"

We fought. Eventually, Kit diffused the situation by telling his mother not to come to Sydney. We would visit with some of the children for her birthday instead.

*

In May 1999 I wrote my poem The Shadow (after Songs of Innocence and Experience, with apologies to William Blake). It was an outpouring that came from Grace's attempt to move in with us in Sydney.

The Shadow

The Shadow has cast its spell, the young lovers cannot escape,
For she has cast her shadow and it will always be there!
Speaks the shadow: -
He was mine first and I shall not let him go.
I have loved him and nurtured him,
I know him too well for you cannot steal him.
My hold is strong, the bonds have been strengthened through his childhood,
For his father and I have trained him well.

I have glimpsed the fire in your eyes,
Yes, you will fight for you are a rebel.
But young maid, you cannot win.
I will break your spirit and reduce you to submissiveness.
Tradition is on my side.
You will fit in and take your place in the scheme of things.
Subordinate your place and there you will stay.

Speaks the proud young maid: -
I have searched a long time for love, to love and be loved.
Someone to protect and care for me
And I shall never be lost again.
The Shadow will not leave us alone.
This fight is not of my making,
But I am grown now and have discovered that I have strength.
I am no longer the lost child of the past,
Then weak and vulnerable.

And what will you fight with, young maid?
Why, with the power of love, of course,
And the appeal to justness and impartiality.
With these I cannot lose, thinks she.
Naive child, you have little experience of the world.
You lack cunning, patience, pretence,
You are intense, easy to provoke, inward looking.
Your virtues become liabilities; courage and honesty
Might do well in the battlefield of old,
But in the hearth, you are poorly equipped to do battle.

But still the young maid fails to learn,
She loses and loses yet again.
Moods and depressions overcome her
But still she chooses to fight on.
She wails "This battle I did not start but I shall finish."

The years pass and they take their toll.
The children came and went.
Her battle with the Shadow wages on, the tempo of which slows at times,
For the children have to be cared for.
Alas, the energy and strength that would have been devoted to the young family,
Have been sapped by the futile battle with the Shadow.
The sparkle has gone from her eyes, and lines tinged by bitterness
Form on her face.
A battle that has done little good
But a battle not of her choosing, she claims.

The Shadow has sown the seeds of discord in the early days.
They have taken root and the noxious weeds

Choke the frail rose bush the lovers planted.

A gentle breeze brings a message as if from a kind, pitying spirit
To the once young maid: -
"Let go of the past and you will be free,
Free to enjoy the rest of your life
Let go, let go, let go ...

Replies the proud now ageing maid:
'No I cannot, I cannot forget the unfairness,
The injustice and the pain.
The guilt I was made to carry;
The guilt that I did not conform to tradition.
That I fought when I should submit
Because I believe that an individual has a right to happiness and freedom.
Freedom from the dictates of others.
For if I was selfish, were they not so?
Why must their interest and wishes always come before mine?
What I did not have as a child, must I be denied as an adult?
I cannot let go for I do not know how!
For I have fought so long, I do not know how to cease.
The turmoil and conflict which have taken hold refuse to subside
And give way to the calm and peace that I yearn for.

Victim, fence-sitter, conspirator?
What was your crime?
You allowed the battle to continue ...
Did you have a choice?
Innocent or guilty?
Could you not have spoken up?

And now you must suffer.
For her eyes, her expressions tell you she remembers.
She pains you with the words she chooses.
She will not let go

Frail of body but sound of mind, cared for by her other child,
Sits the Shadow in her room.
She pleads that she was only looking after her own interests,
As would anyone else.
And the Shadow claims she has suffered too,
For the boy-child that she loved
Is no longer at her side.
He is with the rebel in another land.
Does the Shadow know that the seeds of discord she sowed so many,
Many years ago have borne fruit?
Does she know that victory is hers?

Or is it hers?
For if the young maid of long ago
Is able to let go
The delicate rose bush may yet survive.
The scars would remain like the perennial presence of weeds,
But at least the rose bush will remain too,
If she will but let go, let go, let go …

*

    Grace passed away in 2009. That brought out in Kit a guilty conscience over not inviting her to live with us. Grace's death did not stop our quarrels over her. In one particularly bad argument he accused me of making up stories about her. It still hurts me deeply that, where his mother was concerned, he did not believe me.

Our quarrels were very civilised. I was in deep anguish, but we always respected each other. There was never any swearing or cursing, nor any insults. I just tried to convince Kit that his mother was hostile to me, always unsuccessfully.

*

Twenty years later I wrote The Rosebush. It shows how, reflecting upon my husband's later suffering in health and passing, my feelings towards Grace changed.

The Rosebush

It does not thrive
Yet it does not die.
Three little branches are gone
But the main one is strong.
And a large red rose emerges.
The two remaining branches give small blooms,
The bush survives.
Is this the state of my love?

He is gone.
It has been a month and five days,
I have grieved every single day.
I weep in silence.
I cannot stop the tears from flowing.
I weep for what I had,
For my inability to appreciate what I had,
For the pain I caused you,
For the unwillingness of the two foolish women
To compromise.

The Shadow is gone.
I cannot forget what she caused me.
Nobody won,

Leaving only pain and misery.
I needed to step aside, away from the hurts.
If only I can turn the clock back.
Can I follow the good you stood for
For the rest of my life?
Instead of regret and pain
Can I forgive and accept
What has gone?
But still I do not have you.
Can I carry on with life?

You fall down again and again.
Your body fails you.
You feel that you still have so much to give.
You enjoy the company of those around you.
You loved life.
Your body gave you so much pain. Your body said no.
Slowly it gave way
Yet no complaints came from you.
You kept it from your family,
From the Shadow too, as she continued her demands.
She did not want to know, nor to understand.
She faithfully stuck to her desires.
She left her Shadow to haunt us.

You stood steadfast to your beliefs,
To wife and mother.
Your wife felt you could not understand.
You were the only one always …
Because she received no love, had no one,
You were everything to her.
She placed a burden

Too hard for you to carry.
She knows that you will forgive her
Because that is you.

Yet when night comes, there are
No soft breaths,
No soft coughs,
No warm hands waiting to be clasped,
No nothing ...
But there is still a rosebush.
The dew that falls on the small blooms glitters in the morning light.

*

It is strange that my thinking has changed in the last months while writing these words. Have I finally faced the truth by reliving the past? Did I make a wrong decision by staying with Kit?

I did have happiness. I must be thankful for what I received and never have regrets. I enjoyed abundant blessings and must never forget that. I must accept whatever comes in the next life. Yet now in 2022 I must face the truth. I am also ready to tell the story from my own perspective.

Little Li, without parental love, without even toys, for many years living a childhood punctuated by abuse and fear, grew into a young woman with deep feelings of worthlessness and little self-respect. Even so, I somehow developed a strong moral code, based on both Chinese traditions and western values. My only lie was to pretend to the world that I came from a loving home. And a loving relationship was what I sought.

Unfortunately, the effects of the trauma overtly caused by MahMah and passively instilled by the neglect I experienced as a child resurfaced when I was faced with Grace. It took a great deal of bravery for me to stand up to her, but I knew I had no chance of independence otherwise. Yet I had never learned how to manage people or manipulate situations as she, and many other women, did, so was always at a disadvantage. Being the respectful person I was taught to be, I instead internalised my frustrations, which expressed themselves outwardly as anger and internally as depression and severe gastric ulceration.

To be fair to Grace, she had no idea about the truth of my upbringing: the beatings, neglect, and, after PaPa's death, the poor nutrition. Nor was she aware that my family had been wealthy, and that I was used to a hefty allowance from the family business. Even Kit had only a vague idea about the traumas I had endured. But I am sure that Grace did not have the capacity or compassion to deal with someone like me in any way other than as she did. We were destined to clash.

But my clear conscience and ability to sleep at night comes from knowing that I never did anything to harm Grace or traduce her reputation, even though I had no respect for her. Love and goodwill, a resolution to never harm others, these have carried me through my life.

13 Australia the first time around

Melbourne, 1967

The lock of my vanity case has been broken and my few items of jewellery removed. I have never owned much jewellery. The most expensive item was the single large deep sea pearl and sterling silver chain that I wore for my wedding, a present from Ah Chieh. Was it stolen on the Malaysian side or at the Australian end? The discovery is made when I claim our luggage in Melbourne that December in 1967. But there is no time to moan over it; there are three little children to look after.

The three children are all under six. Also with me is Ah Yoke, my girl Friday, almost sixteen, a gem who helps with the kids. No, we are not migrants, not yet. We have no thoughts of migrating. This is to be an Australian adventure and then it will be home again to Malaysia. Kit had left Kuala Lumpur for Australia two months earlier on a two-year training scholarship from the Malaysian University Hospital. He went to New Zealand for the first part of the examination, although the departmental head was keen only on the training. However, Kit decided to sit for the exam as well.

It is with relief and joy that we meet Kit at the airport as we come through immigration. He soon loads us and the luggage into a Holden station wagon. It has been most exhausting getting the children through a nine hour night flight, plus two hours getting to the airport and through the immigration formalities. All I want is a bed, a nice soft bed to lie on and sleep forever and a day!

Kit drives us to the attractive home he has rented. While I make for the children's bedroom, dragging the boys along to put them to bed, Kit goes straight for the TV. Is the Australian Prime Minister found yet? He has disappeared into the surf and the chances of him being found alive are growing slim. We arrived on the day that Prime Minister Harold Holt has gone missing!

Who could have predicted that a Prime Minister would go missing at the beach?

The next one and a half years is a good time for me. Melbourne represents a beautiful, free Australia. Life is good for the average person. There is violence and crime, but ordinary Australians are hardly affected. Most non-Anglo migrants in Australia at that stage are Italians and Greeks. There are few Asians. We see Chinese migrants only in Chinatown, around Little Bourke Street and in the suburban Chinese restaurants. Melbourne is peaceful and quiet. When asked where we are from I never fail to say we are visitors, in Australia for two short years. We receive no nasty remarks and are never shouted at, see no racist unpleasantness, although I had heard and read there was a dark side to Australian society, that there was racial discrimination.

I am getting to enjoy life away from Malaysia. There is no intrusion by relatives, no one to give unwelcome advice, no one to tell you that they have eaten more salt than you have eaten rice, therefore you should do as you are told! In Australia you are encouraged to use your own judgement. I enjoy the quiet and peace, the respect for my privacy, although I miss the intimacy of my siblings, for there is much caring in Asian families too. But there is also much emphasis on blood relationships, reminders that blood is thicker than water when demands are made on you by your family. Such appeals can be over-used and abused. I resent such intrusions into my life. In Melbourne I enjoy my freedom. I feel that Australia has much to offer. After a year I ask Kit whether there is a chance of our living here in the future. Kit's reply is "No way, I have a mother to look after at home. We have such a good life in Malaysia, why would we go anywhere else?"

Here I am in Australia, still young at 27, still so eager to live, not yet aware of life's ironies and how lucky I am. I have three beautiful children, healthy and lively. I had bad morning sickness during my pregnancies, but everything else had been fine. Childbirth was a breeze. It was only years later I learnt that I had a medical condition which left most women infertile – a retroverted uterus. This is actually a treatable condition, but that was not known at the time.

The first Christmas in Melbourne is magical. "You say yes, I say no, you say stop, I say go, go, go …". "Yesterday, love was such an easy game to play … I believe in yesterday ….". The Beatles' voices ring out in the shopping centres. We take the children to Christmas displays in department stores at the city centre and to Chinatown for Chinese food. On most Sundays we go out for picnics at the public gardens or a scenic spot. One Sunday we go to the new National Gallery of Victoria building. I recall the family lying on the carpet looking up at the ceiling, which is made of stained glass. Kit and I watch the children roll about and squeal in delight! They love their Sunday outings. We have a good family life.

A musical interlude

Cool Melbourne weather in 1968 finds us at the Domain Parklands, seated on rugs on the ground while the three kids roll on the ground with blankets on them, listening to Australian pop music. The performers are The Seekers. It is a magical night. Judith Durham's voice is so pure as it rings out through the wintry air. The others play their instruments and sing harmonies. It is wonderful music and good lyrics. There are no gimmicks, no fancy additions, for none are needed. The memory of that night clearly remains in my mind although it is so long ago.

The Seekers was the preeminent group for me and Kit in our enjoyment of western music. We loved the Beatles, Simon Garfunkel, the Bee Gees and so many others.

An episode of a cat that loved curries

The attractive house that Kit rented came with a cat. We were not cat lovers, but the house was too good to turn down. The cat was not bad looking either, the pet of the landlady's ten year old daughter. They planned to go to England for two years, while we planned to stay in Melbourne for the same amount of time. It was a good fit. The landlady was originally from England. Her house was well kept, and I felt that one could expect her to do everything well, as she appeared to be the efficient, no nonsense type. She was not keen on young kids, but since Kit had assured her they were good children and that the house would be well looked after, plus we were willing to look after the cat, she agreed to rent the house to us. One benefit of the house was that it was in a quiet area in Glen Iris. A greater attraction was the big park with swings at the end of the road, only five minutes away!

The house had a formal dining room, which we agreed with the landlady was out of bounds to the children. At the back of the house was a good-sized playroom, which suited the kids, and which was why we agreed to ban the kids from the dining room.

The landlady's instructions were that we buy liver (at our expense) from the local butcher every other day and feed it to the cat. It was extra work and cost. In Malaysia domestic animals ate what the family ate. Malaysian families were also curry lovers. Kit's bachelor friends were always hungry for Chinese food as well as curries, so we often had friends over for meals. Ah Yoke found that the cat would eat Chinese food. One day Kit bought a big fish and we had a lot of curried fish leftovers. Ah Yoke and I gave each other a wicked grin. Feed the cat with it! It would mean saving the cost of the liver and the labour of cooking it. But the cat sniffed his dish and turned away. Well, we tried.

Two hours later I took a look at the cat's bowl and what did I see? It was licked clean! Kit came home to hear sniggering from the kitchen. He soon joined in the laughter. The cat had a new name, with the children calling out "Curry cat, curry cat".

From curried fish the cat graduated to chicken curry and beef curry. Its appetite had also grown, and it was eating more.

The children and the cat got along well. Curry Cat loved to curl up next to our little daughter.

Unexpectedly, the landlady was back after only a year. She asked for her house back. Kit felt we could not deny her that, although I was concerned about the children. They were happy and settled. Our older boy was in Year 1 and our second son had entered play school. We would have to find new schools. How do we find a house with a playground that close in a good area? We had two weeks to find a new place.

We handed back the house after a close inspection. The landlady found a small rust mark at the far side of the mirror in the formal dining room. She claimed it was not there before. Ah Yoke said she had seen it when we moved in. The landlady dropped the matter since the cat had been well looked after. Indeed, the cat was healthy, if heavier, but its coat was sleek and its mewing sounded fine.

Three days after moving out we had a call from the now ex-landlady. She was worried, as the cat was refusing to eat the liver dish she cooked! I replied that it could be sick or missing my children. In truth, the cat had become a "curry cat", but how do I tell her to feed it curry! Kit found me and Ah Yoke in hysterics when he came home from work. On learning the cause he could only grin!

Back to studying

Meanwhile, I had not been idle. My first choice was to study, finances permitting, otherwise I would get a job. Two weeks after arriving in Melbourne, once the children were settled in, I was at the University of Melbourne's Faculty of Education. There were courses not available in Malaysia. A lovely lady of Indian origin helped me with my enquiries. She told me that a librarianship diploma would take no more than a year, while a master's degree in education may take longer. She told me I looked reliable and hardworking, and they needed an extra pair of hands: would I consider working with her? She would train me. I told her I needed to talk things over with my husband and would give her a reply in three days.

Kit and I had to discuss our finances. His pay was in Malaysian dollars, our costs in Melbourne were in Australian dollars. Could we afford for me to study instead of get a job? Kit was never one to shirk work and he had plenty of initiative. He found he could do locum work on Saturday mornings. The additional Australian fifty dollars bought a week's meat at the wholesale Queen Victoria Market. The children did not eat that much – on the top of our short grocery list was the three bottles of milk they consumed every day.

I was a capable money manager and never overspent. In fact, I felt that I spent more freely as a child than in my married life. Grace had repeatedly accused me of extravagance, but I knew I was frugal. Other than my cheongsams for special occasions and one suit I did not have any new clothes. I had been given two second-hand thickish dresses and a skirt for the Australian winter. A good friend also lent me a leather jacket, and that was my best and warmest piece of clothing. After we returned to Malaysia Grace asked for my winter clothing for one of her nieces. She did not believe me when I told her I did not have any. They were either returned to their owners or worn out!

I turned down the job offer and ended up at the Royal Melbourne Institute of Technology doing a librarianship course. Kit had assured me we could manage, and I should not miss the opportunity to study if I were so inclined.

It was an enjoyable time. Every morning I drove to the station in an old beetle Volkswagen and caught the train to go to lectures. I took my lunch: two hard boiled eggs and a bottle of water. Sometimes I would treat myself to a coffee. It was only after I completed the course, when I started working, that I bought lunch, usually a pie or a toasted sandwich. One of the best things that happened to me at the RMIT was meeting classmate Dawn. She was of Canadian origin, and her family had settled in Australia. She soon got to know Kit and the children. She and her boyfriend loved our Chinese food and Malaysian curries.

Whenever lectures ended early I would rush home to my children while Dawn, still single, would study in the library. Generous Dawn would share her notes with me. I have been so fortunate with friends!

My time in Australia had been so enjoyable that, when faced with migration in 1976, there was little hesitation in choosing Australia. My brother Yeh elected to go to Canada, as did many Chinese from Hong Kong as well, because of its enlightened racial policy. The United States, the most advanced country in the world, was of course attractive. But for me it had to be Australia.

In my time in Melbourne I had no arguments with Kit. It is hard to believe, but true. We laughed together a lot. All I wanted was to be a good wife and to enjoy our time with the children. I can only remember being unhappy on two occasions. The first time it was only briefly. Both times it had to do with Grace.

Grace had written me a letter of reprimand when she learnt that I was not working but doing a librarianship course. She accused me of selfishness, indulging myself in study when I should be working. I should be earning a graduate teacher's income and helping Kit instead of letting him work alone. How dare I make such a decision! I had, as always, she wrote, taken advantage of Kit's kind nature. What I should do now was to quit the course and find a job. That was her order. She probably felt she had the right to do this as she and Kit's father had paid my first university fees. The reprimand stung, but she was not there physically. Besides, sister-in-law Chun had also written, sending her encouragement, even offering to lend me money if needed!

The second incident was more significant. Kit received a photograph from Grace. I had not realised how much a photograph could tell.

The photo was one of Grace at her most attractive, as she was slim then and looked charming. Around her cheongsam collar was a necklace. This was what caught my eye. It was my favourite necklace! A very pretty heavy pink glass necklace. I had packed it with some gold wedding jewellery in a drawer in Grace's house. She had offered me one of her three drawers for items I did not wish to take to Australia. In the large drawer was my wedding dress, two favourite blouses, letters Kit wrote to me during our courtship days, all the things that were precious to me. They had been carefully tucked away. Grace was English-educated and knew the meaning of privacy. She had been on a six month visit to the United States on a grant from the Methodist church in the 1950s and had travelled to a few other places. She claimed to be knowledgeable and widely read. Why did she not give me due respect?

She had gone through my belongings. Surely a person's personal possessions should be left alone. She knew I would recognise the necklace. Was it her vanity that led her to send the photo? In the earlier years she had often told me that she was very beautiful when young and had many suitors. Or was it deliberately to infuriate me? She knew I did not share my possessions. She saw that I had some attractive expensive blouses sent to me by my aunt in Hong Kong and approached me to allow her to wear them. I refused. She was at least two sizes bigger than me, although I wore my blouses loose and she wore hers tight. I had given her the bottle of Chanel No 5 that Kit bought me, as she kept using it. I did not want to smell like her, nor did I want her body odour on my clothes!

I pointed out to Kit that my privacy had been invaded. To Kit I was being petty. What harm was there in letting someone use my things instead of them lying in the drawer if it gives the person some pleasure, especially his beloved mother?

Nine years later, in 1976, a similar incident happened. We had moved to Ipoh and I was again offered the use of the same drawer. I found that the prettier of the two new cheongsams made for me in Kuala Lumpur (where my favourite tailor was located) had disappeared! I had only left them there the previous month. I learned that Grace had given it to her favourite niece! Her mindset had not changed. She had the right to my possessions. She had a right to run my life …

Last months in Melbourne, 1969

My little daughter escapes through the back gate and a neighbour has found her standing on the tram line! The kind lady brings in the two year old. I am inside the house. Ah Yoke is in the backyard, hanging out the washing, and took her eyes off the toddler only for a few moments. She normally stays close to Ah Yoke or me! We are shaken, and cannot risk it happening again. This old house is located in the poorer part of Toorak, too close to the main road.

Kit takes immediate action. We are off house-hunting again. We find a better place, although it has been badly neglected. However, it has a good-sized front garden and a large backyard that is safe and ideal for the children. Most importantly, it is away from the busy street. Ah Yoke and I do a big clean up to make the house liveable. The former owner was an 81 year old lady who had moved to a nursing home.

Our oldest and youngest children play quietly on their own. Our middle child feels neglected and is mischievous. Of late he has taken to pulling his sister's hair. That brings plenty of attention but ends up in his hand being smacked. The week of my library exams he upsets me by pulling his sister's hair again, and I have to smack him before I set off. He looks at me, his large eyes filled with tears, but he has to be disciplined, and that is how it is done in those days. He is five years old.

One evening Kit and I lock ourselves in the bedroom to study for our exams. Son number two decides to play cowboys and Indians, which he has been watching on TV. He is the young brave leading the charge at the fortress (our bedroom). He leads the other two in banging and bashing the door. I, the fortress commander, have to sally forth and deal with the brave leading the attack!

The year ends well. Kit not only passes the final examination, he shares the top award with the leading scholar amongst Kit's fellow students. I tell the children that their PaPa has done very well in his exam and the children clap for him. Kit beams with pride as he looks at his family. We are happy.

Kit receives the results in the morning and I have high hopes of being taken out for dinner. Just the two of us. However he has other plans. He asks for two blankets and two pillows. Why? He is driving off with good friend and fellow golf nut Michael for a three day golfing holiday at nearby country golf courses. To save money they would sleep in the Holden wagon. Sorry, dear wife. The passionate golfer has been missing his game.

Both of Kit's golfing mates, Michael and John, were given their English names by their Aussie friends. Kit's workmates have not been successful in giving him an English name. They suggested Peter or David. Kit preferred a version of his Chinese name. I, too, stick with my own name, which is much easier to pronounce than those of many other immigrants. Our thinking is much the same: we are who we are!

Early 1969 sees the children get more treats. They do not have to wait for "uncles" Michael and John to bring them ice popsicles and lollies. I have found a library job, and there are popsicles in the freezer and snacks in the pantry. The job is at Essendon, near the airport. My boss was one of my lecturers and I am lucky to have been offered a position. It is a long drive in my nine year old VW beetle. But first I send the boys off to school, as I had done from the beginning. School is nearby and Ah Yoke walks them home. Six weeks later, I find a library job much nearer home, only 12 minutes away, so I have more time for the little ones.

Summer ends. Autumn starts. The notorious Melbourne flies disappear and so do the warm days. We remember our first winter in Melbourne. There had been coughing and vomiting as the flu stayed with us for six weeks. Nobody escaped. Our first house had no central heating, and neither does the current home.

What can we do to make the place warmer for the children? Time for a serious discussion between me and Kit. Do we buy a good heater? I am working and we can afford it. There would be no objections from our landlord, who lives next door. He is Australian Chinese, local born, with an Australian wife. His three children are just a bit older and play well together with our three. He appreciates our improvements to the house.

Kit comes up with a new suggestion. Why wait for the end of the year? Why do we not go home? He has already trained for a year and a half, the minimum time required. The department will welcome him back, as they can always do with an extra pair of hands. I have gained a new qualification. We can avoid another cold Melbourne winter. For me, the memory of Grace's hostility has also grown dim, as I have not seen her all this while.

So we went home in May instead of October or November. Yes, we were back by 13 May 1969, with no thought that we might risk our lives. Death was just around the corner for some ...

14 Politics in Malaysia, 13 May 1969

Political developments had been taking place in Malaysia while we were in Australia.

The government was led by the Alliance Party, a coalition of Malaysia's ethnic groups, under the leadership of prime minister Tunku Abdul Rahman. The leading power, representing the Malays, was the United Malays National Organisation.

The ethnic Chinese community made up 38 percent of the population, and was represented in the Alliance Party by the Malaysian Chinese Association (the MCA). Ethnic Indians, represented by the Malaysian Indian Congress, accounted for more than six percent of the population. Together, they held the economic power in the country.

By 1969 the MCA was seen by many in the Chinese community as useless, only good for toeing the line.

New parties such as the Democratic Action Party and the Parti Gerakan appeared, campaigning for a "Malaysian Malaysia", for the equality of all Malaysian citizens. Their success in the general elections of May 1969 was such that they nearly took power.

The politics of 13 May 1969 was complicated and no mere "incident", as it was later described. It was a time when truth became a casualty. There was finger pointing, with the Malays on one side and the Chinese and Indians on the other.

While my focus in life was my husband and children, I was not unaware of the political situation at home during our absence. I was not privy to, nor do I have inside information about, occasions when Chinese killed Malays, the full role of the Chinese secret societies, or when elements of the army and police killed the Chinese. The following is my strong recollection of the Malaysian political situation in May 1969, including what I saw, heard and learnt.

Death was just around the corner

General elections were held in Western Malaysia on 10 May 1969. The MCA candidates did remarkably well, despite the agreement within the Alliance Party that only allowed them to stand candidates in 33 of the 104 constituencies. The Chinese candidates won almost every seat for which they stood. For the Chinese political party it was a brilliant triumph. Victory parades went through the streets of Kuala Lumpur. There were Chinese supporters who flaunted the victories and taunted their opponents. A most unwise act in a multi-ethnic country!

A Malay strongman had emerged, deputy Prime Minister Abdul Razak. Behind him were senior political figures, realists who feared the worst for the Malays. There were extremists hovering around as well, opportunists too, but the most dangerous were the religious ones. They were not afraid to shed blood. One extremist was Dato Harun, who was the chief minister of the state of Selangor. Kuala Lumpur, the capital of the country, was in his constituency. Many sources trace the racial riots to him.

The Malay extremists' argument was that this was a crucial time. The British, when they granted independence to Malaya in 1957, had left political power in the hands of the Malays. But now the Chinese were threatening to dominate, and the 1969 election was the proof. Kuala Lumpur was falling under their control. If the power of the ethnic Chinese went unchecked, the Malays could end up second class citizens in their own country!

There was also another source of danger according to the extremists. Two hundred miles south of Kuala Lumpur stood newly independent Singapore with a predominately Chinese population, led by popular Lee Kuan Yew.

For the extreme Malay political leaders there was to be no more stalling, it was time to act. The Malays still held the trump card – control of the army. The army was overwhelmingly

Malay in composition. Few of the other ethnicities had been allowed to enlist in the army. There were other favourable factors, the gun issue to start with. The communist insurrection in the days under the British had led to the banning of guns in Malaya, and that law had never been repealed. Malaysia was a gun-free society. The British had also banned the communist party. Dangerous Chinese extremist elements were dealt with.

Such is my understanding of the Malaysian political scene at that time.

*

Back to my family. Our return to Kuala Lumpur was much easier on 8 May 1969 than our arrival in Melbourne had been. The difference was Kit. My hero could manage everything! When necessary he could carry a child under each arm plus organise everything. He had communicated with his bosses, so we were to stay in a hotel for five days and then move into rented quarters. To my delight, we headed to the classy Majestic Hotel from the airport.

On 13 May we moved into university rented quarters at section 16, Petaling Jaya, a newer area away from crowded Kuala Lumpur.

We spent the morning unpacking. Getting the children's beds made was the priority. After lunch they had their afternoon naps. Thank goodness the hot Malaysian weather made them sleepy. Kit arranged for delivery of the box of our household items stored in his cousin's garage. We still had time, so we tackled that. We got to the barbeque, set bought shortly before we left for Australia, and opened it up. Light brown cockroaches, dark brown cockroaches, speckled cockroaches, small ones, medium sized ones, large ones, see how they run! I have never seen so many cockroaches in my life. I hate cockroaches! "Please don't run up my body!" I ran screaming into the house. It was just as well that we had unpacked in the backyard.

We had an early dinner and Ah Yoke helped me put the children to bed. Kit and I had another shower to get rid of the dirt from unpacking. It was still early, not yet nine o'clock. We gave each other a meaningful look. Oftentimes we could read each other's thoughts. Yes, we wanted supper. Not any supper, but beef balls and rice noodles from the Kuala Lumpur town centre!

For a year and a half Kit and I have been dreaming of this yummy dish. The middle-aged couple who made them was the best known in Kuala Lumpur. The beef balls were not only delicious, but they had a chewy and crunchy texture. They were accompanied by a fantastic chili sauce with just the right amount of vinegar to give the dish a tangy flavour. I told Kit that I wanted a bowl of rice noodles with twice the number of beef balls. Kit said he wanted two bowls. We headed down to the garage for the car. In forty minutes we would be feasting. Not so …

Our new home was a short distance from the major road junction. At the traffic lights we needed only to merge to the left and we would be on the federal highway. Then it was straight down to the roundabout next to Kampong Kerinchi and from there on to Kuala Lumpur's centre. As we approached the traffic lights we could see three cars awkwardly parked at the side of the road, but there was no one at the scene. I said there might have been an accident, so we should investigate in case help was required. We parked at the roadside and walked towards the cars. The first had a shattered windscreen, and the driver's door of the second was smashed, but we could not see any damage to the third car. Strange that there was no one around!

Then came the sound of a scooter behind us, steered by a young Indian boy with an equally young Chinese pillion rider. They stared at us and the Chinese boy blurted "Why are you out here?" Gleefully, I replied that we were going down to Kuala Lumpur for supper.

"Don't you know what is happening? There are racial riots and slaughtering by the Malays just round the corner at Kampong Kerinchi and in parts of Kuala Lumpur. At Kampong Kerinchi there are Malays with parangs [long knives usually used for cutting grass], hunting for Chinese and slashing them. Women are not exempt. Go home if you value your life!"

Kit and I could hardly believe what we were hearing. We got back into the car, turned it around and headed for my brother Kwok's house. He would be able to tell us what was happening.

We drove though the quiet streets, our car being the only one on the road. At the house gate Kit and I called out for Kwok. It was a while before a figure appeared, followed by another. It was Kwok and his wife. A strained soft voice said "Don't you know there has been a curfew declared by the government since 7 pm? There are racial riots in various parts of the city. It is a one-sided attack. The Malays are slaughtering the Chinese, who have no way of protecting themselves. Quickly, return home and look after your children."

Slowly things sunk in. We had moved back from Australia just days ago and had no TV or radio. It was inconceivable that someone wanted to kill us because we are Chinese!

Kit and I rushed home. Ah Yoke and the children were safe. They were fast asleep.

Realisation dawned. Had we not stopped at the lights to investigate those three cars we would probably be dead. To get to the supper place we would have headed down the federal highway and passed Kampong Kerinchi, where there was a small Malay village. A mob had rolled petrol drums across the highway. Anyone looking Chinese was stopped and attacked. Kit and I looked too Chinese to escape. Three little children would have lost their parents!

Two angels of mercy had appeared to warn us that death was just around the corner. Who were they? Why were they on the street when a curfew had already been proclaimed two hours earlier? Were we meant to live?

We discovered that there was a breakdown of law and order. The compassionate Prime Minister Tunku Abdul Rahman had collapsed in tears when he learnt what was happening. He loved his citizens and could not understand the hatred and the killing!

The official casualty figure was 500 dead, then raised to 700. I heard that the real figure was 5,000. The General Hospital in the city centre was said to have been overflowing with bodies, people dead from slash wounds. Sister Chien had stories from Chinese sources. Apparently the Chinese secret societies, the only civilians with guns, had come to the rescue. They had rushed to the areas where the slaughtering was taking place. Their shots caused the attackers to scatter, guns proving superior to the parangs. But soon it was their turn to run, for the army was called out. The secret societies could not withstand the superior fire power.

Aftermath of 13 May 1969

The fear and tension caused by the May 13 killings lingered. Rumours were rife every day. The population was urged to ignore them on the radio, TV and in the newspapers. Regardless, shopkeepers often closed their premises early, while street hawkers rushed home with unsold food. Life was more important than profits.

The first exodus of educated, affluent Chinese began. Those who had witnessed the killings or were told of it by friends or relatives felt there was no future for the ethnic Chinese in Malaysia. If it could happen once it could happen again! These were people who had never before thought of leaving the country. It was not an easy decision. I know they agonised over it, as we did eight years later.

May 13, was, of course, traumatic for us, but at that stage Kit said no to migration. He made me a javelin to place by my bedside for protection. There were times when he was on night duty and not home to defend the family. I was not going to be killed without a fight, and Ah Yoke also kept a big wooden pole next to her bed.

*

I met and spoke to a few politicians in the 1960s. In 1961, as an elected student representative, I met Lee Kuan Yew, the President of Singapore, sitting three seats away from me at the same table at a University Chinese dinner. I managed to make the points the student body wanted raised: that our university roads needed care and good maintenance. That funding was important. I was too shy and in too much awe to say more.

In 1964 I met the fourth Sultan of Pahang on more than one occasion, as I was the doctor's wife in the royal town. As etiquette dictated, I invited him to dance the joget (a Malay dance). A tall regal figure, he was imposing and gracious. The Sultan treated Kit well, played tennis with him, and allowed Kit to ride his polo ponies.

In 1969 I met Prime Minister Tun Abdul Razak. In exchanging the Malay greeting, a quick touch of the hands, I found his were cold but that he had a warm personality. As we did the joget I told him my father-in-law was KM. They had struck up a friendship years before in the state of Pahang, when Tun Razak was a young man at the beginning of his political career. KM had been a friendly older adviser. Indeed, he remembered my father-in-law, as well as his two children. He wanted to know how the young Kit and his sister Chun had fared in life. It was not a cold, aggressive politician I met, but a kindly, warm person.

*

May 13 also affected my domestic life. I planned to employ a cook/housekeeper as well as Ah Yoke, as I intended to go out to work. But Ah Mui, who had previously worked for both

Grace and me, was not part of my plans. Her loyalty was to Grace. In my opinion she was cunning and unscrupulous, treating me as an outsider.

I had already interviewed a professional Black and White cook/housekeeper and made arrangements for her to start work. It was Kit who let on to his mother that I was getting a new employee. This led to a showdown.

Grace told me she needed to talk to me seriously. She started by telling me I was being stupid employing a stranger. Next she asked whether I wanted my children murdered. My new employee was Chinese, so it was nonsense talking about a hostile Malay woman murdering my children. She demanded I re-employ Ah Mui, who would rush back anytime. (And why shouldn't she? I paid well and allowed her to eat as she pleased.)

Grace emphasised that times were uncertain and we needed people we could trust. Besides, Ah Mui was a good cook and could produce Kit's favourite dishes. She had been trained by KM. Kit was inclined towards Ah Mui, but did not want to make an issue of it. The final say was to be mine. I did not want to re-employ Ah Mui, but submitted to the pressure. Dire consequences ensued!

Ah Mui worked for me for the next seven years. She gave good service initially, but became difficult, causing me much heartbreak, for she helped create a toxic atmosphere in my home. She was a first class spy and served Grace well. She knew that it was Grace who got her this cushy job.

Every new purchase, household or personal item, was duly reported to Grace. Nothing escaped Ah Mui's sharp eyes. My visitors, including my relatives, were closely scrutinised, while Kit's received less attention.

While we lived in Kuala Lumpur Grace lived nearby. When she came for dinner each evening she received reports from Ah Mui. Grace walked freely into my bedroom to examine my private purchases. Grace kept count of the number of my cheongsams. My flower arrangements were rearranged by Grace. It was her son's house and therefore her house!

When we moved to Ipoh, the first two hours after Grace's arrival were spent in close conversation with Ah Mui. The "debriefing" was taking place! Ah Yoke was my faithful supporter who saw everything. Maybe it was wrong of her to let me know, but she felt for me. Besides, Grace had tried to get me to sack Ah Yoke, for she knew Ah Yoke was loyal to me!

I felt depressed and troubled ...

15 Reluctant migration

Time to say "Goodbye Malaysia"

It is not only me who feels troubled. Problems continue across the country. The relationship between ethnic Chinese and Indians on one hand and Malays on the other have steadily deteriorated. Hardliners have taken over the government. Where English was spoken in schools it is replaced by Malay, now the national language. Students must identify their ethnicity on their examination papers.

Meritocracy disappears from schools. Unexceptional students are pushed through when their basics should have been strengthened and the teaching techniques improved. Mediocrity spreads to the civil service.

Malaysian qualifications are no longer recognised internationally. The United Kingdom is the first to announce it, with the advice to try to improve standards. The reply is essentially "Nick off, we do not need your recognition."

Well-to-do Chinese send their children abroad to be educated. Britain is a popular destination. A British degree means the chance to work overseas or a new home should things turn bad in Malaysia.

*

Did anyone bother to count the cost to Malaysia from the loss of the intellectuals, the brilliant students? At the Victoria Institution's school reunion in 2015, where I did Lower and Upper Form 6, I witnessed much and remembered the outstanding students who studied there at the same time as me.

The former students returned to a very successful and happy reunion in Singapore, only a short distance from the school in Kuala Lumpur. Singapore could almost be home. Two brilliant brothers returned from the United States, while other remarkable students travelled from the United Kingdom, Canada and Australia. These were people who would have succeeded anywhere. The very organisers of the reunion were now Singaporeans.

A rendition of the school song had to be observed. Everyone sang it with gusto, but also with affection, for the students loved their old school and treasured the memories of the carefree years they had spent there. One could feel the sadness when the evening ended with Auld Lang Syne. There was many a teary eye, for would we see each other again? Would there be another reunion?

The realisation came to me in the midst of that sadness that those at the reunion were pushed to leave the country of their birth and their youth. They had not gone willingly, but left for the safety of their families and, like me and Kit, the future of their children. Here were more reluctant migrants, dispersed to various parts of the world!

The British had put great efforts into education and left a good school system in many of the Malaysian states. Two other top schools in Kuala Lumpur were the Catholic St John's Institution and the Methodist Boys' School. There were also outstanding students from the Chinese schools, which received funding from the Chinese business community. Their students also contributed to the exodus.

The reaction from some in the Malaysian community was "Good, please go! We do not need you." They thought there would be more wealth left to be shared by those who remained.

*

Back to our family. Our eldest boy turns 14. He has good marks in all subjects but one. If he does not pass the national language exam, even if he has distinctions in every other subject, he fails the entire year. He and his Chinese classmates develop a phobia about Malay. It is a young language and school classes are not handled with patience. Malay is not spoken or acknowledged in other countries except for Indonesia. New words are introduced every week, only to be discarded and replaced by others shortly after. The government becomes aggressive and tells the population "If you do not accept the policies of the ministers you can leave the country." Things get bad for a while. Local ethnic Chinese are taunted with "Balik China" (Go back to China).

Kit and I were born and brought up in Malaya, now called Malaysia. We do not know China, have never been there and do not write or read Chinese. Even after May 13, we still feel that Malaysia is where we belong, although we were almost massacred!

But it is not a case of Kit and me. It is a case of our children's future. Kit states that we cannot expect the children to be brilliant. We brought them into this world and we owe them a duty. We want them to be free and to live in a country that respects them. If they aspire to be political leaders, so be it. They should not be barred because of their family's origins, nor be thrown into prison for speaking out. On their part, we expect them to contribute as loyal citizens. And so the days pass with us in deep thought and deliberation.

Petty corruption proliferates on the streets. Kit and I drive out to buy fruit from the stalls, as it is the season for the sweet small fruits called langsat. Kit walks over to the stalls while I stay near the car. A policeman hovers over the front of my Peugeot 504. He gives a shout. I am not proficient in Malay, just as he is not in English. He gestures towards the road tax sticker. I remember that I forgot to change it yesterday. He shouts again. Kit rushes over while I am apologising for my oversight. I try to tell him that the new sticker is on the desk at home. Kit patiently tries to explain in the national language. It is obvious the man wants a bribe and Kit refuses to bribe. Kit challenges him, he backs off. We go home with a bag of langsat but a bad taste in our mouths.

A fortnight later I am in trouble again. I rushed out of the house with my second boy and just the car keys to fetch my older son from the swimming club less than 10 minutes from our house. It has been a bright day and it is only a few minutes past seven in the evening. I am stopped by a policeman. He wants to know why my lights are not on. He wants a bribe. My son in the car shouts "Give him two dollars!". But I left my handbag at home, having hoped to do a quick pick up of the older boy.

I relate the incident to Kit. Two such occurrences in two weeks, and he is worried.

Well-to-do locals send their children overseas as early as the age of 12 years. Bad news travels fast. One 14 year old, gone for less than a year, has died of a drug overdose in England. Another has had a mental breakdown and the parents have to take him home. The boarding schools are strict and cold places, and not all young students are strong physically and mentally. Kit feels that if one sends them too early one loses them. Your children become strangers and you do not see them growing up. What is the meaning of family? We conclude that we must stay together and migrate as a family.

We have decided not without pain, for we had never thought we would ever leave this country of our birth and upbringing. There are so many places we love, our schools, our friends, and the members of our extended families. Even the old lady around the corner who has lived in the neighbourhood for so long!

I think of my father, the reluctant migrant. The filial son who never questioned his father. His consolation was the idea that he would one day return to China. For Kit and me, it was a decision we had to make ourselves, and it was final. We would return for visits, but we would die in a new land, our new home. Yet did we have a choice? Am I not a reluctant migrant too?

Leaving Shanghai had been soul-wrenching for my father. What did leaving Malaysia mean for the reluctant migrant's daughter? I feel I speak for many migrants. You do not leave the land of your birth and upbringing without pain. Childhood is a special time in one's life. Regardless of the circumstances there are inevitably times of happiness, tender moments carved into your heart and your mind. Childhood is a special gift.

*

In 1976 many families are thinking of migrating. Kit has talked with his good friend Wan. Wan declares "I will swim or sink with this country." He has assets, we have little. We have no investments, only Kit's salary. Kit has started to earn well. Some friends think he is mad to give up the good practice he established almost seven years ago.

Kit again ascertains that I have not changed my mind. He reminds me that life will not be easy in Sydney. We are a family with four growing children, for I have given birth to a third son.

We decided on Australia as we were happy there in 1967-68. Kit has sounded out his mother. Grace has been living a quiet but contented life with her partner San for over ten years. San has always been supportive of her and they mix with her friends. They have also been travelling, visiting his children and grandchildren overseas. Grace abhors housework and cooking. She declares she will not go to Sydney, except maybe to visit. To live there without domestic servants would be madness for her. She has San, her friends, relatives and daughter Chun around her.

Grace asks Kit to consider migrating to Singapore. It would be easier for her to move in with us there in her old age. Kit still owes her filial piety. But Kit thinks of Australia as the place to bring up the children. He cannot be persuaded otherwise.

Ever since I learnt of the depth of Grace's hostility towards me in 1973 I have feared her. Migrating to Australia will give me the chance to move from her dark shadow. Throughout our years in Ipoh her visits had always ended up with scenes between me and Kit. We tried to confine them to the bedroom. The scenes kept alive the emotional conflict within me and the bouts of depression. Is this a chance to finally break free?

Meanwhile, the hurt my father caused me seems to have lessened over the years of my life with Kit. I watch my parents fussing around brother Sang's children and wish them good luck.

Li's parents, Zhang Jen and Luk May in the mid-1970s

Our last months in Ipoh approach as 1976 draws to a close. Kit makes it known that he is migrating with his family, while others keep their movements secret. One prominent family leaves in the stealth of the night, and even their best friend is kept in the dark!

An unexpected event takes place. We hear that Kit's file in the income tax department has been "moved". Is Kit being investigated? It is known that the government has recruited a dozen competent tax investigators from India. A common complaint against professionals in Malaysia is the under-declaration of income. This could also be used against those who are migrating. They could end up with a hefty fine or be banned from leaving the country. This is worrying for Kit.

Life is strange. Old flame from 1957, Mr Gorgeous, turns up, just as good looking and charming. He is working in the right place. He is also a good friend. I ask him to check whether Kit is being investigated, but he must not jeopardise his position. He knows I am anxious and drops in at our house. He tells me that Kit's file was moved due to some tidying up in the tax office, not because of any investigation. He sees my relief, smiles and tells me I should have married him.

For my last three months I had planned to widen my expertise in cooking, learn special dishes and shop for the array of things I need to take to Sydney. Again, plans are only plans. I collapse. For two months I am in constant pain. I go for investigations. Finally, I am found to have a blood clot in my abdomen. I am operated on and slowly recover. As we approach the date for our departure to Sydney I am still pale and weak.

Sydney, 1977-1979

The children are now fourteen, twelve, ten and three. I no longer have that gem, Ah Yoke, to help me. We have had seven years of easy living in Ipoh and forgotten what Australia can be like, refusing to consider the dark side of Australian society. We forget that life is not a bed of roses.

It is a new existence, with adjustments necessary for all. The young children suffer when we go to Sydney. In Malaysia, the children were always surrounded by friends. Children seldom jeered or shouted at each other. In Asia there is always a lot of respect for others. Our children also learn that there is no domestic help now.

*

Kit migrates two months earlier and gets everything ready for us. The children and I arrive to a beautiful house and a sturdy station wagon. In the mornings we are faced with a traffic jam in the kitchen as the three older children rush through breakfast to get ready for school. The kitchen is much too small. Kit did the house inspection at night and underestimated its size. There is only one solution, but we will have to wait while other matters take priority. Move house, but not yet.

The boys are settled in a Catholic boys' school located 12 minutes away and our daughter in an Anglican school 15 minutes away, leaving one child at home during the day. Trust me to have a hyperactive three year old! One morning he decides to have an early morning sip of coke, so he drags the two litre bottle from the fridge. Oops, it is slippery! I spend the morning cleaning glass fragments from the kitchen floor. The next day he throws two toilet rolls down the stairs, as he wants to see which one is faster. On most days he puts the toilet system to the test because it is fun watching what can go down the flush. Most days I am so tired I could lock myself up and sleep for a year!

Our older boy never fails to bring in the washing from the clothesline. The day he stays late in school my laundry has dried and been drenched again by the afternoon thunderstorm. The second boy is strongly built and helps with the carrying jobs, largely the groceries. Our daughter keeps her younger brother entertained and gives me a break. They all try to help.

Meanwhile Kit is having it tough, too. For starters, Kit is only earning half his previous income. His years of service are not fully recognised. At work, he is treated with disdain by a colleague: friendly and sociable Kit offers his hand in greeting, which is deliberately ignored. Kit is told the guy is South African and not the friendly type. Kit remains open and pleasant and works even harder. My Confucian gentleman (junzi) rises to the challenge and earns the respect of those around him.

After six months we move to a larger house where we are more relaxed and less cramped, but we are also on a bigger bank draft. As a private joke Kit starts singing to me each morning "I owe, I owe, so off to work I go!"

Before long there is a stream of migrants from Malaysia. We are not alone in our convictions. We host six families in our first year. Our youngest son has to share his room with the older boys when a family stays. These are Kit's old and dear friends, although a couple do take advantage of him. The children have a hard time. They are good, and never complain. Kit is busy with work and looking after his friends. He does not have enough time for his own children, or so I feel.

*

A thin officious lady looks at me in a very matter-of-fact way. She coldly states that the issue is my son's case of nits. She eyes me and frostily announces "Your son brought NITS to school." I protest that he must have caught it from his classmates. I tell her that my husband is a doctor, and we have a high standard of health and cleanliness. I have already treated him. She can come to check our home if she wishes.

She shows annoyance and glares at me. "You are Asian, are you not, Mrs X? Your son is the only Asian in his class. The nits can only come from your family."

Yes, I am Asian. I am Chinese. I have never been ashamed of my ethnicity. I was born Chinese, and I have always been proud of being such.

The interview is over. It beggars belief that a person who is educated and holds such a position in the community could have so little idea of how nits spread. What can I do but maintain my dignity and walk away gracefully? I do not believe we have such bigots anymore. Anyway, I hope not.

Another incident occurs around 1980. I receive a bill from the local chemist. Kit started an account for medicines – antibiotics and such. I am surprised to find two items of cosmetics from a brand I do not use. As a rule I do not buy personal items on credit.

The owner, the chemist, is in, and I eagerly inform him that I did not take the creams. Wrong! He sternly tells me that I have been identified by his accountant as being the purchaser. A thin, haggard looking female comes towards me and says "You did take them, Mrs X."

The chemist gives me a wry smile. "I am sorry. You do have to pay, otherwise it gets unpleasant."

I do some quick thinking. I ask them whether there is another client with the same surname. There is. I get her phone number from them. As soon as I reach home I phone her. I learn that she does buy cosmetics from the chemist and puts them on her account. I return to the chemist the next day, search out the owner and tell him of my conversation with their other client. He is quick to say it is a mistake then, and surely I know how easy it is to make a mistake and must have made many mistakes in my life. I protest that he refused to give me the benefit of the doubt, that I had been identified and that was it. There is no attempt at an apology or even a smile. Instead, his final comment is "You Chinese all look alike."

I met this other lady. Believe me, if you care to spend one minute with us you will see that we do not look alike!

*

The boys are in a good school, but we try to get an even better one for them. A couple of "know-alls" start advising us about the schools in Sydney. We are told there is a top school, but the only way to enrol the boys is to board them there. We visit the grounds and are carried away.

We could not have made a worse choice, but the boys do not tell us what is happening.

We find out only later that the school is rampant with racism. Many of our children's classmates have never seen foreigners before. These youths are young hunks at 16 and 17 years, excelling at sports, with little interest in academia. They are fine specimens of masculinity but their thinking is still that of young boys. They are inclined to move as a group, to follow a leader, rather than to act as individuals. Our sons find their clothes and belongings covered with spittle and thrown out of the dormitory windows. The other boys deliberately bump into them when walking to classes.

My second son is well built, but those boys are six footers. He is alone, while they move in gangs and welcome any hint of a physical bout. Racist taunts are flung at him every day. Like his brother, he is called a dirty, filthy Asian. Worse is being told "We do not need your kind in this country. You do not belong, nor fit here. Best that you get lost, vamoose, you are dirt!" To be told as such on every school day for two years, although the first year is the hardest. To wake on a beautiful morning to insults, taunts that get more vicious each day. There is no escape. Every day he runs into them. They continue to inflict pain on him as if it were their God-given right! Each time he is told he does not belong here. Think of the psychological damage on the migrant child. It leaves my second boy with a feeling of emptiness, of being an outcast.

My eldest son is in his second year there, and gets some protection from his tall roommate, who is also the school's vice-captain. My second boy is a newcomer and alone. He reaches breaking point and disappears into the city one day. The housemaster sympathises with him, but it is an issue nobody wants to deal with. It is a hornet's nest!

My sons never complained. Besides, Kit was always busy, busy earning the boys' exorbitant boarding fees. With me it was the housework and the casual teaching I did to contribute to my parents' living expenses. It made approaching us difficult. It was our loss.

My second son, like his father, has a ready smile and a friendly nature. Knowing what he went through after the fact, I am thankful that the two unhappy years in boarding school did not destroy his warm personality. However, sadly, there are repercussions for our older son from his two years as a boarder. In Malaysia his family had been well respected, and he had enjoyed the prestige of being his father's son; his father was someone of worth and social standing in the community. Here he was a young dirty Chinaman, to be despised and taunted. It was many years later that we learnt he believed he had been dumped in the cold and hostile boarding school by his heartless parents. It drove a wedge between him and us. He became a loner, choosing to live in another part of the country.

At her school, our daughter was the only Asian in her class. I remember she broke into tears when a so-called good friend turned on her, rudely saying that her skin was the same colour as poo. She also chose not to complain, keeping much within her. She was a serious student, and it was not surprising that she was the dux of her final year.

At home things happened on a smaller scale. The neighbour's children would come to play and enjoy lollies when there was no one else around to play with. When one of them had a birthday party, my son of the same age was not invited. When the party boys saw him they jeered and laughed at him, shouting "Ching Ching"!

*

Many years later I learned that my youngest son did not escape unscathed from racism either. Like the others, his crime was to be the child of migrants.

He got his "share" in 1984, when he was eleven years old, in his first year at a public high school. The school that his brothers went to turned him down, saying there were no vacancies. Thank goodness for that!

Our youngest son was three when we arrived in Sydney. Over time he discovered chips and junk food and grew chubby. Two Year 10 boys found it fun to bait him, provoke him, call him names and push him about. Both of them were a head taller than our son. He was fun to "play" with, as he was too plump to move fast and made pathetic attempts to retaliate. They looked for him each morning before school started.

Then one morning it got most exciting. The chubby migrant boy took a Bowie knife to school. It belonged to Kit and was kept on display in a glass cupboard. As the tormentors tugged at his shirt, he pulled the knife out of his bag and flashed it at the two bullies. The bullies were shocked but reacted with glee.

This was going to be fun! They rushed to the school office and it was reported to the deputy principal that a Year 7 boy had threatened two Year 10 boys with a knife! Our son was apprehended and the knife taken from him. Strangely enough, we were not called in or informed of the incident.

I had done casual teaching in this school, and the incident was related to me later by a teacher I knew well. The deputy headmaster was neither gutless nor unaware of what happened in his school. He knew that the two older boys were regular troublemakers. The head and deputy masters decided to do their own disciplining. All three boys were cautioned. It was decided that the parents should not be involved. Nobody had been hurt. I do not believe my young son would use a knife on anyone. He has never been in a fight. He simply was not going to tolerate the bullying anymore and he is not a coward!

Melbourne, 1990

Some ten years later, my brother Yeh, now living and teaching in Melbourne, meets with the worst case of racism. Yeh and I are the runts in our family. It is not a problem for me that I am short. Yeh is also, solemn, not the smiling, overly friendly type. He is deadly serious about his job and works extremely hard. His students in Malaysia adored him. Here in Australia, his style of teaching is not always appreciated.

He offends a female teenage student at his secondary school. She is not interested in learning and creates unnecessary distractions. She is told that there are others who want to learn.

The student gets revenge with the collaboration of her good friend. She claims that Yeh dragged her out of the class by her hair while swearing at her. Her friend claims to be a witness. My gentle brother has never hurt anyone physically, least of all a female student. But her parents have gone to the headmaster and want Yeh sacked for gross abuse of their daughter. Yeh is called to the headmaster's office to explain himself. He denies ever laying hands on her, but is asked to resign. It is hard to believe that an experienced headmaster is ignorant of how far errant students can go. Easier to scapegoat a Chinaman!

I taught as a casual teacher from 1978 to 1990. I know what students can be like. While I can appreciate young growing minds, I know also to avoid the few troublemakers. I have thicker skin and am more sociable. After work I also have Kit to laugh and joke with. I am a survivor. For my brother, it was the end of his career.

Becoming Australian

In 1981 we become Australian citizens. We are very happy to have a country to call our own. We hear from the Malaysian Government and are asked to return our Malaysian passports as we are no longer Malaysian citizens. There is no such thing as dual citizenship, nor are we interested in it.

The early years in Sydney are physically exhausting as I had been pampered, being brought up in a country where there is cheap labour. My father was a reluctant migrant to Malaya from China to increase the family fortune. In a way I am also a reluctant migrant, but I moved to Australia for the values my husband and I consider more important than material wealth and physical comfort. We now have our peace of mind and our freedom. We never regret coming to Australia for a moment. We accept the dark side of Australian society with the good.

I stay home for the first year with our youngest child. The next year he goes to school and I find a job doing casual teaching. This gives me an income while leaving enough time to look after my family, although some days are still a physical struggle.

In my experience, casual teaching is never satisfying. Neither students nor fellow teachers consider that you are actually teaching because you are not. You are a babysitter, without the responsibilities of a full-time teacher. You are a necessary evil trying to keep the restless students from running amok on those occasions when their usual teacher is away. I prefer to teach my subject – history, especially Asian history when I get the opportunity. The children I meet of non-Asian background seem to know so little about the Asia/Pacific region and, I feel, should learn something of the mindset of China, India and Japan at the least.

Young minds must be taught never to refuse to learn.

Casuals also have a hard time because students expect to have some fun when their teacher is away. Students bait casual teachers in the poorly disciplined schools in the rougher neighbourhoods. The more foreign the teacher looks, the greater the expectation of fun, it seems. I learn to avoid the tougher schools and accept work at the more disciplined ones. I am also lucky. I search for word games, puzzles and vocabulary-building exercises to use, and these are appreciated. I also keep in mind that I may be twice the age of the students but there will always be those who have knowledge and experience I do not. Australian children come from such varied backgrounds. On two occasions I manage to arrange to teach Asian history to students in their matriculation year. It is voluntary, and I do not need to be paid. However no one is keen on such arrangements and such opportunities are few.

I have news from Malaysia that my father's health has deteriorated and he no longer earns a living. My casual income helps him and my mother. Two of my sisters also contribute, for which I am grateful, as I need some of my pay to dress well at work. I know how important image is. I have seen the school kids make fun of poorly dressed casuals. I brush up my social skills and learn to communicate better so that I do not get bullied.

We settle into daily living in Sydney and Kit gets back to his adventurous self. He joins a local flying club. In Ipoh he had a flying licence and now he has one again. It had given him so much pleasure when he could take the children at the hospital on joy flights.

Kit starts to burn the candle at both ends. He has Saturday golf and his monthly flying, but he is greedy for more. He introduces the family to skiing. I am no longer young, but I refuse to be left out. I take to skiing, undeterred by the cold or the heights. I love the wind on my face and the sense of freedom. Lessons are expensive, so we learn the hard way – through painful falls and sprains. Our holidays are always low budget. My being the cook and launderer helps keep expenditure to a minimum.

Then the inevitable happens with such a high risk sport: I fall, tear a ligament and need surgery.

During my recovery, while limping across the living room, I catch sight of what I consider one of the funniest scenes on TV. A big man holding a ball struggles towards a goal line. Three opponents cling to him, one on his back, one on each side. Still, he manages to cross the line and deposit the ball on the ground. His name is Mal Meninga. Thus is my introduction to rugby league. I descend into raucous laughter. Kit bursts into laughter at my hilarity. A few days later, again there is a big field on the TV screen and one of the most beautiful tunes ring out. It is I vow to thee, my country – my school song, a tune I have loved from the time I first heard it as a child. I learn it is the international rugby union theme song. How can I not take to this game as well? It becomes my favourite.

I also pick up watching cricket from my boys. I learn the names of all the players in the Australian team against England for the Ashes, and many of the English team. The Olympics come around and I yell my lungs out for our Aussie team: "Aussie, Aussie, Aussie, oink, oink, oink" was how I said it. Come summertime again and I consider myself on first name terms with our Aussie players! I have become a sports nut. Life is good.

16 The growing years

Back to the family

At Castle Hill we are too far away from the universities in Sydney. We move nearer to the city, as we plan for the children to go on to tertiary education. Kit has bought a piece of land and finds a builder to construct a six bedroom house. It is a modest home. The children have their own rooms, although they are small and simple. There is also a small guest room for Grandma Grace when she visits. The house includes a large kitchen and huge family room for the children to relax and watch TV. Our luxury is the 12 metre swimming pool, as our daughter is a mad keen swimmer. Kit works long hours, for now he has a bigger bank loan to pay off.

Time passes. The boys are through the worst, which is the Higher School Certificate (the HSC). Our eldest boy gets into medicine. Kit buys him a second-hand car and he drives to university every day. We are still too far away, but we are unable to move nearer as we do not have the funds and Kit works in the suburbs. Kit has never invested before. He has no experience with finance, and we have no one to turn to for advice. His initial forays are not successful, but luckily the sums are not large.

Our second boy gets through the HSC. He selects engineering. Kit buys him a second-hand car and he drives to university every day. His university is nearer than the one his older brother attends. Our daughter goes to a nearby girls' school. She is a good student and well disciplined. I have thoughts of transferring her to a top girls' school, which is quite a distance away, but we decide against it. She is intelligent and a good student and we know she will make it to university.

As expected, our daughter does well in the HSC. She has the marks to enter any course she wishes. Her father's long hours and time away from home make her decide that medicine is what she does not want. She chooses Commerce

Law. Kit does not want her driving in every day and decides she should stay in residential college.

By 1983 we have a good social life. We join a "gourmet" club of five Australian couples and dine out once a month, sampling the different cuisines available in Sydney. There is a lot of choice as there are diverse migrants in Australia. On the sporting side, we join a ski lodge, even though it is not cheap.

In 1984 we venture to Europe to ski. Our European ski holidays for the next few years are low budget. We rent our own accommodation and do our own cooking. Meat is unbelievably expensive in France! We take two legs of lamb and two scotch fillets with us from Australia. If there is a good oven we roast the lamb, otherwise we make curry. After five or six days Kit takes us out for dinner as a treat. Sometimes we stay quite a distance from the ski lifts, and it is hard work trudging through the snow in heavy boots with skis balanced on our shoulders.

17 A portrait of conflict – love and hate

My father is dying of cancer. I return to Malaysia and sister Mei takes me to see him. He has lost all his money running his bookie business and does not have the health to continue, even if he wanted to. He, my mother and sister Chien live in a modest rented house. He is a sad sight. He needs to be taken to the toilet. I get ready to lift his frail body with sister Mei, but he waves me away. He does not want me to touch him. My mother rebukes him. "Mei cannot carry you alone, besides, she has a bad shoulder. Li is the stronger one." Yes, I have good muscles. The years of housework and skiing have made me fit.

Now you are dying, my father, your rejection amuses me. It is consistent with your attitude towards me since I was 13 years old. It has happened. I no longer hurt as before. I have toughened up and accept that neither of my parents care for me. No more crying and pleading for attention after so many years of pain. I regard that as an achievement. This is the last time you reject me. I say goodbye but have no more tears for you.

*

Life is strange, an enigma. Zhang Jen had so little and so much to do with my life. My father helped to create the damaged, emotionally disturbed child Li.

Li was only little but her heart was big. There was so much love in her. After realising that Jen was her father when she was five, Li longed for him to show her some affection. A touch, a pat on the head, a smile. Even to just call out her name. Why did he love some of his children, but not Li?

At twelve Li was a confused child, both negative and positive. But not everything was lost, for she also had resilience, the desire to excel and a spirit of adventure.

Many years later I came across a photograph of Jen's mother in her late thirties. Of the girls, Li resembled her the most! Did he notice that? Did he not love his mother? He disliked me the most. I do not understand …

I loved you, my father. I remember the occasions I was with you in the very early years. They were happy times, the autumn and spring festivals and the Chinese New Year. I was so proud to have your eyes and eyebrows. I wanted to have your nose, like Yeh and Mei, but mine was broader like my mother's. I wanted to be completely like you. When you returned to the shop in 1953 after four or five years in Singapore, I was barely thirteen years old and still longed for your love. My classmate's mother, who dropped me at the shop after a day's play at their house, remarked that my father was a very good looking man. I always knew that.

My father had no love for me. I think that I did not measure up to his traditional standards. I had developed so much independence living in the shop because no one looked after me. After Ah Chieh left I had no attention from anyone. My parents and I were strangers. I think my mother found it uncomfortable when I stared at her and she avoided me. Perhaps my father did not like me looking straight at him, trying to make eye contact. He probably interpreted it as boldness, an act of defiance, not becoming in a female child!

I was soon in trouble with him. My father had a habit of listening to our conversations. It did not matter that I was chatting to a guest in our shop. Our visitor was a boy from Singapore who had been my parent's neighbour. My father did not like the way I was talking. He walked right up and swiped me across the face with a heavy right palm. A red mark immediately appeared, but I felt the shock he inflicted, rather than the pain.

Within weeks of hitting me, he was to hurt me again, this time with his words. It must have been a Saturday morning, for we were not in school. A middle-aged English customer was in the dressmaking shop, one of our old faithful customers. She noticed me often, and, pointing to me, remarked to my father that he had a pretty daughter. In a loud voice, in broken English, my father replied "This one no good, this one bad, the one inside, that one good." He gestured to

Mei, who was further back in the shop. The lady rapidly pointed out to him the look of dismay on my face. Not that it ever seemed to worry him what my feelings were!

My father, why do you pick on me? Your absence of affection is one thing, but to hurt me physically and mentally is unnecessary. You add to my feelings of inadequacy, that I am of little value, instilled by MahMah. You further injure the damaged person I have become. I am not included in the outings with your favourite children. Brother Yeh is not included either, but you do not hit him. I am the only one you strike.

I learn to stay out of your way. We live in the same building, but not on the same floor. My meals, shower and bedroom are all upstairs, yours are on the middle floor. You rarely come upstairs and I do not see you for days at a time, but you are to hit me again.

Mei and I are invited out to parties. I am not into parties, but Mei is interested. I go because I get to chat with others, and it is less boring than staying at home. We sneak out, as our father does not like it if we mix with boys. One evening we go to a party. Although it is only ten o'clock, I decide to leave and get a lift home. Mei chooses to stay. As I emerge from the toilet I bump into my father who has come upstairs to check on us. He questions me as to where Mei is. Why is she not home? I am one and a half years younger, not my sister's keeper. I tell him that I do not know. I am standing at a slight angle to him and do not see his blow coming. His right hand lands heavily across my neck and shoulder. He turns away and makes his way back down the stairs.

I am crying quietly in my bed. It is the psychological impact on me. I am so detestable I need to be beaten. I am that unimportant piece of turd, destined only for prostitution, as MahMah has told me many times.

My mother does not touch me. She avoids looking at me and refers to me using a nickname I detest. My parents share their dislike of me.

I continue to live upstairs. The dry cleaning shop is still a going concern. It covers the food bills and I continue to get an allowance each week. MahMah's opium addiction gets worse and the caning ends in 1951. She is subdued and kinder to me these days.

In school I am full of life and playful. I pretend that my parents dote on me and that I am a treasured child. At night in bed I am melancholy, sometimes weeping silently.

I have a third unfortunate encounter with my father, which I strongly believe could have ended disastrously for me. Brother Sang and I are having an argument when our father comes upon us. Sang lives on the second floor with them, but sometimes comes upstairs looking for fun. My father starts to rebuke me, for he apparently has no hesitation in deciding I am at fault. He does not bother to find out what the quarrel is about. I have had enough and run up the stairs in tears, but must have my parting shot, for I am a fighter. I fling out the words "Of course it is your favourite son quarrelling with an outsider, who is a nobody to you!" He is infuriated. I can detect his raging anger when he shouts "Come down this moment to receive your punishment!" I was not born yesterday, and know my father's poor control of his temper. An inbuilt protective mechanism kicks in, and I take to my heels, scooting off as fast as I can, without shoes, running down the stairs on the OIC side of the building and out into the back lane. I fear for my life, but I am a runner in a school team and he will never be able to catch me.

I find out later that, in his frustration, he catches hold of Sang and thrashes him instead. It is the first time in Sang's life that his father had beaten him. My mother refused to talk to me for months, as I had caused her favourite child to be beaten. I watch my step, not venturing anywhere near my father. That he eventually stopped trying to punish me made me think perhaps he realised how unfair he had been. In later years, sister Meng's declaration that our father was a very biased man gave me some comfort.

My school certificate year came with no help from my father. No financial assistance, no lifts to school from him, and I think he did not consider me good enough to sit in his car. With my weekly allowance from OIC I was able to get through the two additional years to matriculate. My mother did not succeed in convincing me to take an office job. I would appeal to MahMah when she tried to force me. But to be fair to my mother, she did not try too hard.

Those years, 1958 and 1959, were the most successful my father had as a bookmaker in the horse racing business. He bought a good sized house and moved out of the shop with my mother, Sang and Chien. Yeh and I continued to live above the shops. Our father had enough funds to help me and Yeh through university if he had wanted to.

I learnt years later what Sang did. The house had been bought in Sang's name. When our father's bookmaking business started to go downhill he sent Sang to the bank for a $20,000 mortgage. Favourite son decided to apply for double the amount. He spent half on a gamble and lost. I only needed M$7,000 for my university education, including hostel fees. That was the sum I accepted from KM and Grace. If my father had helped me then it would have saved me much pain later.

The final rebuke from my father was on my wedding day. I moved from KM and Grace's home to my parent's house the day before the church ceremony. My friends in Singapore gave me a beautiful negligée, but it needed shortening. My younger sister Chien still lived with our parents. The year before Jen had sent her to Hong Kong to do a needlework course. Surely she could shorten the garment for me?

Chien was a simple girl, loved and protected by our parents. She was number seven in the family, the baby. She had never been encouraged to work hard at anything. Chien had hated school, was often sick at exam time and had been allowed to quit after Form Three. Our parents could not bear to see her suffer at school. Chien was so slow at her sewing that she was at it again the next morning. Whenever Chien is stressed she coughs, and our father found her crouched over the garment, coughing. Our father demanded to know what was happening. Of course I was the culprit. He ordered Chien to stop sewing, glared and shouted at me for making her work. Dear God, must I be sworn at on my wedding day?

18 My Chinese Odyssey

After the death of my father I return to Sydney to find I have time on my hands. My three older children are busy with their studies. During my final year of university in Singapore I had promised myself that I would return if I had the time. That year in 1962 had been hard, a mad rush with bad morning sickness and constant fatigue. This time around I would choose my subjects and work at my own pace. I wanted to major in philosophy back then, but my father-in-law ruled against it.

There is a good department of Chinese Studies at Macquarie University, not too far away. I would like a better understanding of the gods to whom I kowtowed and burnt incense. I want to study Chinese philosophy for myself, not to earn a living. I consult Kit and receive his whole-hearted support.

I enrol part-time for the first year. I enjoy it and find that it does not take too much of my time, so I decide to go full-time the following year. And a study trip to China is proposed, one I cannot pass up ...

Life as a mature-age student

I enjoy the advantages of being a mature-age student. Firstly, the lecturers treat me like a friend. There are other students like me. I am not the oldest either. I do not have to worry about money. I pour cups of five cent coins into the photocopying machines and bring home stacks of reading material. While in Singapore students fought over the limited reference material, I have little difficulty here. Where I covered only 30% of reference material (partly due to my own inertia) in Singapore, I now cover 90%. I only need to drive three days a week. I eat well at the canteen. I still do two days of casual teaching work a week. I am at a top school. The principal and deputy are kind and professional and I get to know the teachers well.

I sign up for the six week study course in Xi'an with Kit's blessing. A very capable senior lecturer organises the trip every year. Some of my classmates went last year and came back singing the praises of the course. I had not considered it last year as I felt it was too soon and my language skills were too poor. However, now I am in a better position. I have a whole year to prepare, as I do not leave Sydney until December 1985.

I work up enthusiasm for my forthcoming trip. The "Chinese" in me surfaces. Kit understands and gives me space. He even suggests that Grace could come for a longer holiday and do the cooking while I am away. My very capable daughter is 19 and will do the marketing and the laundry. Kit plans to eat out more often, so that the cooking load is not too heavy.

For the rest of the year before the trip I try to do what I can for Kit. He has been so kind and generous. He is more knowledgeable about history than most husbands I know. I always take pains to explain things to him. Less known incidents in history, odd facts and humorous events. At times, he has been so convincing in his relating of historical facts you would think he had done the research himself. His sense of humour always made it enjoyable to tell him funny things, too, and many times we would collapse in laughter.

After all these years I failed to realise that Grace could not cook. True, she always had the services of a good cook, but it is a revelation, nonetheless. Kit had not known either. I found all this out when I returned. Her dishes were swimming in oil and the meat was too raw. My daughter took over the kitchen. I had thought Grace so knowledgeable, as she often talked of making good Chinese soups and the use of spices. She also spoke of the family recipes, as my father-in-law was a very good cook.

Grace had also become bored and already returned to Malaysia before my trip to China ended.

Xi'an

We are fourteen university students, four of us mature-age, from Sydney, Melbourne, Adelaide and Perth. I am glad to learn I am not the oldest. After a flight to Hong Kong and a three day train trip we arrive at our destination on 30 December 1985. I am exhausted but thrilled, after the long and harrowing journey, to be in the ancient capital of various Chinese dynasties, but best known for the Tang and Chin. Xi'an, city of the Entombed Warriors!

I share a room with my classmate Mel, in one of two spacious bedrooms adjoining a large bathroom with a toilet and long bath. Two quiet and pleasant nuns share the other bedroom. They do not wear a habit, but are in normal clothes. The Foreign Language Institute of Xi'an is our home for six weeks. The grounds are large, the dormitories unbelievably big. The rooms are clean with solid, comfortable, good-sized beds. It is winter and we have two blankets each. There is a large desk, a more than adequate lamp and a sturdy chair for each of us.

Li at her desk in the Foreign Language Institute of Xi'an

We are told that the dormitories were the most modern at their time of building, meant for Russian teachers who were to help with the education of Chinese students. But they never came. I recall reading about the split between China and Russia. A time when the Russian experts left in a hurry, taking with them the blueprints of all their projects, including those that were not completed.

We are well fed. Food is plentiful. Breakfast is more than ample. There is rice plus various dishes for lunch and more elaborate meat dishes and rice for dinner. Only one person complains and she is being unreasonable, as we pay very low fees. I would have to talk to her and remind her of this. It is my job to keep the peace, having been appointed to this role by the group leader, our senior lecturer. He had accompanied us but is visiting other parts of China for some of the time. He had approached me to act as group leader, or rather, trouble-shooter, as there are always issues to deal with. It is an unenviable position, but I take it on, as I fear there might be problems from the hot-headed young Australian students in our group. I believe I understand both cultures. I am in-between.

A party welcomes the new batch of students on our second day. There is ballroom dancing and the teachers take to the floor. Whenever there is dance music, Kit never fails to dance with me. I miss him and feel so homesick! It is my most miserable New Year's Eve. I go to bed sad.

I get over my homesickness. Home in Sydney is, of course, more luxurious, but I had been prepared for six weeks of the simple life. I had not come on a gourmet trip, but to see one of the great civilisations of our world and the home of my ancestors.

The course is well planned and soon we are into the swing of things. Every morning we walk through the cold from the dormitory to the lecture rooms, but it is no hardship as they are nearby and I am comfortable in my Ugg boots.

Xi'an city is inland and extremely arid. Thick dust coats the leaves on the trees, bushes, hedges, everything. Spitting is common, as throats get dry and often need clearing. Out in the little town one needs to watch where one steps to avoid a slide and fall. I become pretty good at this and have no such accidents. My dancing, especially the quickstep and cha-cha-cha, should improve!

The bus journey into town fills an afternoon. Xi'an reminds me of the Chinese towns in rural Malaysia. There are many little shops, often selling the same things: brooms, dustbins, buckets, toiletries, provisions. There are many eating stalls. One modern-looking restaurant is famous for selling Kwei Fei dumplings. I see a huge Chinese wok frying some kind of dumpling on the street with a sign saying it is Muslim food. I learned that many Muslims have migrated here from Xinjiang province.

I am with a classmate, and we travel to and fro on the bus. We have to stand all the way to the Institute. My classmate is a redhead. She has a most uncomfortable trip back, as two young Chinese girls stand very close to her, staring up her nostrils. Redheads are not common, standing out even in Sydney.

*

I find myself busy with a culture problem. Our young students do not behave as our hosts expect. In Australia students are accustomed to questioning their lecturers, sometimes in a manner that is challenging, even rude. They do the same here. The placing of feet on a desk is most offensive and this happens once. I caution my classmates.

Then an unusual incident arises. A rat has been caught and tied to the kitchen door. The rat is tortured and its squeals soon reach us. Our students find this cruel and demand that the kitchen staff release the rodent. The kitchen staff are upset. I remind our students that we are in China, not Australia. The locals' behaviour is their time-honoured way of keeping rats away. We can explain that what they are doing is cruel, but we cannot demand the rat's release. The decision is for them to make. To me, China is an ancient kingdom, a civilisation second to none, and must be given due respect.

However, there are many happier times. We expected to spend our evenings studying, but the Chinese students come looking for us after dinner. They want to practise their spoken English. They are 15 or 16 years old. Always polite and pleasant. I get to know a few of them well. Many evenings are spent talking with them in English.

We also have little gatherings of Australian students in our dormitory. We find that Serge is a good dancer. He does the Cossack dance, which soon becomes a favourite with all of us. There is gentle sweet Lucy, with whom I exchange massages. We both have aching shoulders. Other foreign students are also staying at the Institute, and Pierre, who is French, often turns up with his accordion.

Lucy's roommate, Barbara, is always cheerful and singing. Her favourite song is John Denver's Sunshine. I am reminded of the morning sun coming into the classroom as I hear Barbara singing.

One evening I cut the hair of our Korean classmate, who had been complaining unceasingly. I had taken some lessons while still in Malaysia. I am slow for lack of practice, but I know what to do. She has so much hair it takes time to get through it. Luckily, I brought my cutting scissors. Next evening more people turn up. On the third evening there is a queue. Of course, it is free. Pierre tells me he has watched me cut and it is good enough for him. But Pierre is too late, and I do not have enough time!

*

The course proceeds well, and within the fortnight we have been on two excursions. The first is to the tomb of the Jade Princess. This is a discovery of recent years. She was found to be very well preserved and covered in a jade suit. By the time we visit the body was deteriorating from exposure to the air.

Her hair had started to fall out. But the visit gives me great pleasure, my first to a tomb.

Pit 1 of the Entombed Warriors, Xi'an

The second visit is a bigger treat. It is to the Entombed Warriors. The scale leaves us speechless, and we learn that there is so much more yet to be excavated. We spend time gazing at the Warriors, dazed and in silence. What is there to say? This one visit will last me a lifetime!

It is halfway through the course. My roommate, Mel, leaves as planned. She has a job waiting for her and felt that half the course was better than nothing. Mel was the noisy one, always dropping things. I am not unhappy, as I can enjoy the entire large room and the quiet. The two nuns next door are easy to get along with. They do not expect me to do Mel's share of the bathroom cleaning, and I just continue with my share.

Some of us are invited to the family homes of the Laoshis for lunch – Laoshi being the title of a respected teacher. I get more invitations because I am the group leader. My favourite is Huang Laoshi, who has been helpful from the beginning. I am invited several times for lunch. I am introduced to his wife, daughter and son. His homemade wonton pastry is second to none.

Out of ignorance, I do them an injustice. Australian cash is popular and I have not needed to go to official currency exchange services in town. Kit had ensured that I have enough cash on me. There is little to spend on until Chinese artists come with their paintings and I buy many as gifts to take home. In return for his hospitality I offer Huang Laoshi Australian cash in exchange for local currency to pay for my painting purchases. Unknowingly, I have calculated a higher rate. I had somehow got the impression that, when using cash, one got a better exchange rate. Mrs Huang soon discovers this at the bank and discreetly asks to return my Australian dollars, saying she had some problems at the bank. I return them the Chinese currency, still unaware of my mistake. Bless their souls. They have given me the benefit of the doubt. They continue to invite me for lunch. I am met with so much kindness from Huang Laoshi. He presents me with two books of Tang poetry when I leave.

Li and Huang Laoshi

What I remember best about Huang Laoshi is our conversations. My standard of Chinese was too poor for good conversation, but using simple words he could make me understand him. On one excursion he pointed out the direction of Hua Mulan's tomb as we pass by. As a child I had heard of Hua Mulan. She was the legendary Chinese military hero who led troops to war and had been victorious while disguised as a male.

More interesting were Huang Laoshi's tales of Yang Kwei Fei, one of China's four great beauties. She was the beloved concubine of emperor Xuanzong, last of the Tang dynasty. The emperor was so besotted with her he would send horsemen thousands of miles south to bring back her favourite fruit, lychees. The lychees had to be eaten as fresh as possible, so many horses and men died of exhaustion on the hazardous journey back. And for good measure, Huang Laoshi included the modern day story of pilgrimages by young girls to Yang Kwei Fei's tomb to collect the surrounding dirt for mud packs to beautify their faces!

I recall one amusing lunch at another Laoshi's home. There was the usual enjoyable dumpling lunch and interesting conversation. What was more entertaining came afterwards. They lived in a busy part of the town and afternoons were even busier. Mrs and Mr Laoshi escorted me to the bus stand, which was already crowded. Each holding one of my arms, they heaved me onto the bus, pushing strongly, as there were others also trying to get on. I must admit that, without their help, I could not have boarded the bus.

Yan'an

I am so excited when news of a three day trip to Yan'an reaches me. Many years ago I read about the Communist Party of China's Long March of 6,000 miles, which had ended in Yan'an. There the members had rested, reorganised and later surged forth once more to end with one final campaign all the internal wars of China.

I quote the words of a Red Army Veteran from the book *China, The Long March* by Anthony Lawrence:

"Night marching is wonderful if there is a moon and a gentle wind blowing. When no enemy troops were near, whole companies would sing and others would answer ... We made torches from pine branches or frayed bamboo ... At the foot of the mountain we could look up and see a long column of lights coiling like a fiery dragon up the mountainside."

The battle-wearied tattered army saw beauty in their efforts. I am not a communist, but I find interest and joy in the human spirit, in those who dare dream when faced with obstacles in life and can see beauty in even the most dire of times.

My two nun classmates and I find ourselves in a bus heading up the mountains. It is not a ride for the faint-hearted. So many times we think the coal trucks will smash into us as they pass with only inches to spare. My classmates wonder aloud whether our bodies will be recognisable should the worst happen. I tell them I firmly believe that our time has not yet come.

We arrive in Yan'an physically and mentally exhausted. It is the Chinese New Year period and a song and dance sketch is on at the hotel. We watch with weary eyes. The hotel is clean and comfortable. We sleep well and wake, rested, early the next day. At breakfast there is an array of little dishes and the best man tow (baked buns) I have ever come across. What a nice welcome!

I eagerly await the car that takes us to the highlight of our trip, the Date Orchard, residence of the revolutionary leaders. I stand before the rooms of the leaders, each displaying the photograph of the man who stayed there.

The big photograph outside Zhou Enlai's room shows him and his wife. The rooms are locked but we can look in. There is the simple double bed, desk and chairs. I linger there for a long time, for Zhou Enlai was my hero since I first learnt about him. He held his own against the western diplomats who sneered at him and China. He stood firm against his opponents within China. His acts of compassion for the common people during the cultural revolution, his love for and protection of the arts at the risk of his own life, all these stand out. He was the only one who Chairman Mao dared not take on. Even Madam Mao feared him! The students loved him.

I am not China-obsessed, for I am also a child of western learning. In my early student days I admired Winston Churchill, Anthony Eden and other British political figures. Later it was John F Kennedy for both me and Kit. I read western authors by the dozen and always had a book in English by my bedside, while I could not read Chinese.

After looking through the Date Orchard we sit on the stone stools in the garden outside. There are two stone tables with a chess board carved into the top of each and four stools to each table. A guide tells us that the revolutionary leaders would sit there most mornings and play a game of Chinese chess. I do something to lock in the scene and remember it for the rest of my life. Dreamily, I move to all eight seats in turn, spending a few moments on each. My two classmates give me a quizzical look. I say to them "I sat on the seat that Mao Tse Tung sat on, the seat that Zhou Enlai sat on, the seat that Deng Xiao Peng sat on, the seat that Zhu De, the military genius, sat on" and so on. My big thrill is that I am where they had been. I touched the same things they had touched. My sense of history is satisfied.

Next we are taken to the cave dwellings. The Japanese had made various attempts at bombing Yan'an, but with little success. Everything was spartan, but casualties were minimal as the caves had protected the inhabitants. It is good to see these dwellings.

The journey back to Xi'an is less hair-raising, in bright daylight and with far fewer trucks.

Xi'an again

We are well past the half-way mark of our study trip. There are many film sessions to help with our listening and speaking skills. The films are in black and white, quite old and poorly lit.

I find them boring. The long hours spent watching would have been more productive if we had face-to-face sessions with our lecturers.

I find an interesting hobby back at the hostel, playing table tennis with my newly found friends!

Now, in 2022, they must be in their forties. Back then, I saw these two eleven year old boys playing table tennis early one afternoon while I was walking back from lectures for lunch. I approached and asked if I may play. They graciously consented. My game was atrocious, although they did not seem to mind. The next day when I headed back for lunch I found them waiting for me. We played about half a dozen times. They had the pleasure of smashing ping pong balls at this Huachiao (overseas Chinese) lady and beating the daylights out of her! I should have got them to teach me to do a decent service.

Li and her table tennis friends

The end of the study trip is approaching. For me it has been a wonderful experience. I feel flattered to have been approached with a one year teaching contract, although they know I have a family back in Sydney and am unlikely to accept.

The administrator had offered me twice the pay offered to my classmates. I do not know whether they are aware I am a senior secondary school teacher. I know that I have much to offer, and believe that I bridge the western and eastern worlds. My Chinese language skills, although still sub-standard, are well above the level of my classmates. I should advance rapidly if I stay. But how can I? I have a beautiful family waiting for me back in Sydney.

As January comes to an end the days seem to rush past. It is early February and time to leave Xi'an. I am sad to go, but ready to move on to Shanghai and then a reunion with my husband in Beijing. It has been an experience of a lifetime for me. This trip to the land of my ancestors is such an emotional journey.

I want to see where my father was born and grew up, where he spent his carefree childhood. Seeing Shanghai means so much. Had he not migrated would I be a local there now? So many died, not only from the Second World War, but from the long periods of internal chaos, war lord rivalries, gangster control and simply sickness, poverty and cold. The country had seen so much internal conflict and been subjected to so much international bullying in the 19th and 20th centuries. To suffer humiliation on its own soil when the entrance to the best park in Shanghai displayed signs banning Chinese (unless attending foreigners as servants, and well-dressed at that!) and dogs.

I am to take an 18 hour overnight train to Shanghai. Classmate Peter will come with me, as he too wants to visit Shanghai. I could not wish for a better companion. Peter is a good, serious student, the same age as my second son. As we leave the grounds of the Xi'an Foreign Languages Institute I see two figures performing a sword dance. How could I have forgotten to inquire about it? I had been fascinated by the dance since I was a child and loved the sword movements. I loved dancing and had always danced well. There had been so much to do and so little time ...

Shanghai

I make my arrangements for Shanghai while in Xi'an, calling my aunt's husband, a solicitor, who draws up a program for me. I had never before communicated with the Shanghai relatives. My parents had never encouraged it. I am booked at the Huachiao Hotel for three days, where my parents had stayed before. I plan to meet up with my youngest brother, Hoong, and his wife and son.

On the train Peter and I have berths in a cabin for four. We want soft beds and an air conditioned room, and certainly no repeat of the tough ride we had when we first arrived, but we have to take whatever we can get.

We find two American girls already settled in when we get to our cabin. I take the lower bunk, Peter takes the upper. The girl in the other upper bunk is very sick, coughing and sneezing continuously. I turn to face the wall and believe I have enough immunity. Throughout the six weeks there has not been a sniffle from me. Back in Australia I have always been healthy, otherwise Kit would not have let me come. I am wrong this time. I have been racing around too much and am run down.

I arrive in Shanghai feeling absolutely terrible. Normally, I would have started on antibiotics. Kit had loaded me with sufficient supply for two people, plus everything else including treatments for cuts, headaches and colds. I hardly used any myself, but had foolishly divided up everything and given them to the classmates who stayed in Xi'an and those going on to work in other states. These were expensive Australian drugs they would not be able to buy in China. I had not thought of myself. How could I get so sick in eighteen hours?

Peter looks after me and manages my luggage. My suitcase is not heavy, as I had also given away most of my clothes filling it instead with gifts for home. We make our way to the Huachiao Hotel, where we have booked a large room to share. I spend the day sleeping. Peter contacts my relatives for me.

The next day I am still weak but mobile. Peter does his own exploration. A cousin picks me up and takes me to my grandfather's house. So this is where it all began!

It is a large brick home. It must have been the largest in the area when he was there. This is where my father and his three sisters grew up. My sister Mei and brothers Sang and Chien had lived here for over a year back in the late 1940s, but I am the first and the only one of Jen's seven Malayan-born children to see this house as an adult.

Li in front of her grandfather's house in Shanghai

My cousin tells me that my grandfather would sit under a pergola of grapevines, catching the breeze and enjoying the view each evening. Cousin says that the land around, as far as the eye could see, had belonged to him. Grandfather was also far-sighted. He was supportive of the new communist government and surrendered all his land, retaining only the house. This he did in the very early days of the new regime. He had hated the disunity, corruption and poverty around him in the years prior to 1949, but there was little he could do.

Apparently his surrender of the property was recorded by the government and he was never punished as a landlord. It was also recorded that the land had been bought with money earned overseas.

I spend time inside the house, which I am told will be sold soon. The family will move to a modern home with running hot water! I am shown my grandfather's dark timber double bed. The bedhead is intricately carved. It is very well done and would be considered an antique. I can only caution my sister-in-law not to sell it cheap.

This morning I meet my youngest brother for the very first time. He is some nine years younger than me. Hoong is a big young man, broad shouldered and fairly tall, having inherited our father's build.

Hoong and Li at their grandfather's house in Shanghai

Hoong was the eighth child of Jen and Luk May. The only one of us born in China, he was doted on by his grandfather. Hoong remained when the others returned to Malaya, Jen's gift to his father.

Luk May had complications giving birth to Hoong. She almost died and needed a hysterectomy. When she left Shanghai, Luk May had the comfort of seeing Hoong as a healthy baby, breast-fed by a young nursemaid. She was also reassured that he would be cared for by his grandfather and other close relatives. Hoong never left China, and Shanghai was probably the only place he knew.

I can see that Hoong is moved to meet me, the first of his siblings he has encountered. I am also touched. The family resemblance is there for all to see. Yes, he has the same large Zhang eyes and dark eyebrows.

Hoong has brought cash in an envelope. It is from his last pay. He addresses me as "fifth sister" and is quiet and subdued. I am told that he suffered a mental breakdown during the cultural revolution. He had been dragged from the university into the forced student marches. I hear that he is sensitive and serious and lacked the mental toughness needed to weather those turbulent times.

My cousin tells me that her university education was paid for by my father and he had given financial support to many a relative there.

I am taken to the city and fix my eyes on the streets. So this is Shanghai, where all the excitement took place! Shanghai, the Paris of the East, where foreigners roamed freely, where gangsterism was rife and where nightlife was abundant. Shanghai, the bastard child of China. Here in winter the wheelbarrows had rumbled down the streets with men calling out "Bring out your dead." People who had died during the night, too sick and poor to survive the cold Shanghai winters. I must have been only ten when my father had related this scene, not to me, but to his older children. I had been hovering around. I heard and I remembered!

I also think of and honour Zhang Yu, who had worked so hard and realised his dream. He had gone too early to consolidate his gains. The little child Li had loved him too, and he was seared into her memory.

I go with Hoong and his family to the home of my aunt and her solicitor husband for dinner. I meet my aunt's family. On the next day I am taken to lunch at the largest Buddhist temple in Shanghai. Peter is invited as well. Here are stored some of the earliest Sanskrit scripts, brought from India centuries ago. It is a beautiful temple with many engravings, and the vegetarian meal is delicious.

Li at the Bund, Shanghai

One morning Hoong and his family take me to the Yu Gardens. Hoong insists on paying, although I would have preferred to save him the expense. My mother's sisters visit me at the hotel. I call my mother in Malaysia and they take turns to chat with her. I can hear her excitement, for her voice becomes very shrill!

I wish I had known my mother better, but she had little time for me. I know so little of her childhood, her parents, or her sisters who I have just met. We had the time to talk in later years, but I was still too hurt by her neglect. She was humble and far from self-centred. Her conversations were never of herself. She was so different from Grace. She had suffered when Ah Chieh joined the Zhang family, but carried herself with dignity and never complained.

A Portrait of Luk May

Luk May played the role of the traditional wife to perfection. She was supportive of and submissive to her husband. She never raised her voice or showed any bad temper. She was the ideal spouse and completely devoted to Jen. He came first, there was no other man for her. Had she been widowed while young, I do not believe she would have allowed another man to come into her life.

Luk May, 1935

I also believe she had better brains than my father. She was educated but had left school to marry him. It was an arranged marriage. Her Chinese script was good and her characters were beautifully written. She was humble and modest. I also remember that she was known as the Shanghai beauty in our neighbourhood. One old family friend told me that he and some other young fellows would peep at the young Shanghai beauty at the shop, as, in the early years she could be found helping to tidy the displayed goods in the mornings.

Although she did not bond with her sons, apart from Sang, Luk May loved and doted on her Zhang grandsons. Sang let her down and used her for his own selfish needs, but Luk May's daughters treated her well. Meng was always generous and Mei would visit. And even though little Li had found herself rejected, I always sent a portion of my teacher's salary to help Luk May and my father.

My sister Chien had much to tell after Luk May departed this life. I learned that Luk May realised she had "backed the wrong horse" by estranging me. That made me laugh aloud! But Chien also said that our mother had been most unhappy with Grace's complaints about me. Each of their meetings had ended with a long list of my flaws. How dare Li ignore the wise and sound advice of a kindly mother-in-law? Luk May would apologise profusely for not having taught her daughter well. She apologised for being a poorly educated person, unlike Grace, who was so worldly-wise and well-educated. Could Grace kindly forgive her and her daughter? In my mind I thought of my mother as the Lady of a Thousand Pardons.

Chien said that Luk May finally decided not to visit Grace anymore after Meng told her it was about time she defended her daughter instead of apologising for her. The two ladies did not meet again during the final decade of their lives. They died within a week of each other.

Luk May lost a leg in a car accident in her mid-fifties, but accepted life and was at peace when she passed away.

Even though I did not know her well, in retrospect I realise that my mother's unquestioning devotion to her husband was the model for my own approach to marriage and parenting. Regrettably, to the detriment of my relationship with my own children.

More Shanghai

Shanghai is a bit of a daze, as I am not fully healthy. Hoong's wife asks for permission to use the full-size bath in our hotel suite for her son. They use Peter's toiletries! I know they must be puzzled by Peter's presence, but I am lucky to have him looking after me. Our relationship is that of classmate and friend. I do not have to explain. (I am no dirty old lady!)

For the last night in Shanghai uncle has, at my request, organised a reunion dinner with the relatives. There are three tables of ten. Uncle knows the restaurant owner and gets me a good discount. Uncle tells me it would have been five tables had all the family been around. Some have moved to jobs in Soochow and Hangchow. I am introduced to everyone at the dinner but my head is in a whirl. How am I related to each one of them?

My three days in Shanghai come to an end. Peter goes his own way; I head for Beijing. I am beside myself with excitement about seeing Kit.

Beijing

It is a joyous reunion with Kit in Beijing. I always find truth stranger than fiction and there is so much humour in life. But, my beloved husband, how did you get the garlic stench on you? What did they feed you on the flight? I almost gagged when you hugged me!

When I catch sight of Kit I wonder how I could have left him for two months. In the hotel he makes me take antibiotics straight away. There is no reprimand for my foolishness in not putting my own safety first. I feel safe and secure. Kit gave me the space that I needed and I have had my adventure.

It is the first time in Beijing for both of us, and the city does not disappoint. The Imperial Palace is our first target. We return to the hotel exhausted, however with no choice but to return for a second day. I am surprised to find the private rooms in the Imperial Palace so small. Nevertheless, so much history took place there, so much intrigue between the eunuchs, the Confucian scholar administrators and the court cliques led by the princes. It was all still happening while my grandfather was a child. My great-grandfather must have worn a queue (pigtail), as it was mandated by the Manchu authorities, although hated by the Chinese population.

Statue of Sun Yat-Sen as a schoolboy with a Manchu queue

Kit and I walk through the palace grounds. There are many sight-seekers around, mainly Chinese. We do not see westerners, probably because it is still winter. We come to the Marble Boat, a show barge restored in 1893 at the order of the Empress Dowager Cixi. She had cancelled the Chinese government's order for a modern fleet built in the United Kingdom and is said to have diverted the funds to restore the Imperial Summer Palace instead. The Japanese Government, forward-looking and aggressive, picked up the fleet for a song and used it to defeat China in a naval battle against China.

We visit Tiananmen Square, the huge public space where the anniversary of the revolution is held. Each year, the soldiers and military might of China go on display here. We queue to enter Chairman Mao's mausoleum. Our queue is given preference, as we are foreigners. We see the embalmed body of Chairman Mao.

We are booked to see the other celebrated monument of China, the Great Wall. Kit climbs up while I stay low. My chest is painful as I breathe, for I have not fully recovered from the infection. (That American girl must have had really powerful bacteria!) However, I can do what I intended to satisfy my sense of history: I run my hands along the bricks. These bricks, laid so many years ago by the labourers, touched by the soldiers who guarded the wall and who knows how many other people. I walk as far as I can go, feeling the bricks all the time. (A thought occurs to me, what if this section was repaired not long ago?) I plan to return in the future.

Kit has organised a hospital visit. He is keen to witness Chinese variations on procedures that relate to his specialty. We spend a morning at the hospital. That evening we meet with the three doctors Kit had observed, and the administrator who arranged the program, at a good restaurant known for its Szechuan food. We have a delicious spicy meal.

Soon it is time to leave Chinese soil. Goodbye! I return to Australia. I do have a good life here!

19 More travel

Back to Sydney, 1986

Some months after my return from China I get a call from Serge in Melbourne. Yes, classmate Serge, the Cossack dancer from Xi'an. He offers me a job as interpreter to the Minister of Mines. There is a labour problem on Christmas Island. The workers are Chinese and Malays. Serge recalls I came from Malaysia, so I would be ideal for the job. Serge, you flatter me. I have seen top interpreters at work, and I am nowhere near any of them. If I work very hard I might just manage. Besides, I am basically lazy and cannot be running all over the place working as an interpreter. I do not need the work, as Kit earns enough. If I need extra funds I still have my casual teaching. The main reason I refuse is that I owe Kit too much. I am happy just being his wife.

Another year passes and I finish my Chinese Studies course. I get my Australian Bachelor of Arts degree. I have coped as a wife and mother and simultaneously enjoyed my studies. Where to now? I am not blind to the fact that my Chinese language skills are still not good enough. The study course is but a stepping stone. I have to continue if I want to attain some degree of proficiency.

The university department head, who is my lecturer in Chinese philosophy, suggests I enrol for a master's degree and do a research project on the early Chinese migrants in Sydney. My place of study would be the graveyard where the migrants are buried! My work would be to trace which part of China they came from, visit their village and find out more about their origins. Besides having to work very hard, there are potential setbacks. Will my supervisor have enough time for me? I assess my position. I am in my forties, not a young energetic student. I am not brilliant, either. Who would want to waste time on me? Meanwhile, developments take place in the department, where there is bitter rivalry for the faculty chair. I am approached to take sides. I know who is more capable. Both candidates have been kind and helpful, but I do not believe I have the right to interfere.

I make a mistake. I am on the threshold of getting to know the Chinese language well, but am not willing to give my all. I have a good marriage and need time for my husband. He is still adventurous and active. I want too much. Faced with the problems in the department, I decide to withdraw. Yet I still want to study, so enrol for a master's degree in history, which I still love. I return to the university, but to a different faculty. I remain a jack of all trades and a master of none!

The skiing years, 1987 - 1988

Kit adores skiing, so we go to Europe each northern winter. Our eldest boy is not interested. This year he graduates in medicine and the rest of us go with another family to ski in Austria. One morning our friend brings out his new cine camera to film each of us. It is my turn and I veer towards the soft snow at the side of the slope. Clever thinking, but there are others of the same mind. I do a competent turn and the soft snow feels good. I am looking down, checking that my skis are close together, but I suddenly see the sky and do a 360 degree turn, landing heavily on the snow. It is all caught on camera. A blur of a racing skier hits me at speed. He is a youth wearing a helmet and should not be practising on slopes crowded with recreational skiers.

I am lying face down in the snow, my body trembling and my face in pain. Son number two runs for my husband. Kit turns down the rescue people's offer of help and their stretcher. He and our son help me as I slowly ski down the slope. Ha! He graciously accepts the profuse apologies of the young racer's father, making it known that he is a doctor and well capable of looking after me.

Kit gets me back to the lodge. I am moving on my own two feet, although dazed and hurting. He puts me to bed after giving me pain killers and a sleeping tablet. I have tremors for 24 hours and a badly swollen face. The third morning Kit takes me to the slopes. I am skiing once more – cautiously. Kit says that if he did not bring me back I might not want to ski again. He tells me I have got guts and that he admires me! That is my reward, as it is not easy to get a compliment from him! I survive.

Skiing, fun and games

We have money to travel abroad to ski, although our trips are always on a tight budget. Until the late 1980s we went to Europe. France and Austria were the cheapest for skiing, then we moved on to Italy and Switzerland. Kit was always trusting. He was told that it was cheap to ski in Europe, to avoid the USA as the costs were exorbitant. Besides, the US dollar was always so high. It was not until 1989 that we discover that skiing in the US is superior in every way! Food is cheap, too.

Our last European trip is to Switzerland and I fit in one week in Egypt on the way. Egypt, land of the pharaohs, a country to which my love of history had introduced me. I count the days until we leave.

We see the sights in Egypt, the pyramids, Abu Simbel, Luxor, Valley of the Kings and more. The treasures of Tutankhamen are dazzling and rate two visits to the Cairo Museum. We are one of four couples, and cannot deny the men a visit to a nightclub. The belly dancing, of course. The buxom dancer chooses Kit's lap to sit on and we get a photograph to remember and laugh over. It is a great trip!

It is not over yet, as we still have Switzerland to come. Switzerland does not disappoint with its stunning views. What is disappointing is that the snowfall is poor that year. The cows grazing on the slopes of the mountains still make a pretty picture, but the skier would rather that the slopes be covered by deep snow.

In 1989 we ski Vail and Aspen, our first trip to the US snowfields. There is no such thing as poor cover, as snow machines ensure that the runs are well surfaced. We do not ski in Europe anymore, but explore snowfields in the different US states. We buy into a ski lodge.

Kit is a good skier. He goes for the black runs. I am at a good intermediate level, doing my dark blue runs, occasionally going on an easy black run that Kit tests out for me first.

Kit (second from left) and Li (on the right)

Accidents are inevitable. It is not us being careless or incompetent but usually the other skier who has over-rated himself. As older skiers we are more cautious. Ironically, this time it is the falls while walking in the heavy boots that cause us problems.

It is the end of the day and the snow is melting. That is the danger time. Kit tears his rotator cuffs going down a flight of steps to the ski shop, injuring both shoulders. He never complains, so I do not realise how much damage he has sustained.

Back in Australia we return to our ski lodge every winter, whether or not the snowfall is good. It is 1991 and we are skiing back to our lodge at the end of the day. My left ski catches a small stone and I fall on my face. I have a suspected facial fracture and a permanent small dent to my left upper cheek. My left eye is swollen, but I am not deterred. Kit does not think it is serious and encourages me to keep skiing. For the next two days I ski with one eye closed. Crazy middle-aged woman!

The falls do not hurt when one is skiing at a good speed. The skis come off when you fall and the soft snow buffers you. In 1992 I tore the anterior cruciate ligament in my left leg. How? Not in a skiing accident, but in a walking accident. I am following the men back to the lodge at Smiggins Holes. Oops, my left ski sinks into the snow, while my right ski starts to turn. My skis do not snap off because I am walking. I can hear a tearing sound in the left knee. I am in trouble. The men dig me out, but they do not realise I am injured! I do not wish to miss out, so I ski on in pain.

I learn some years later, when my youngest son tears both, that he has "weak" anterior cruciate ligaments, apparently inherited from me. My layman's understanding is that many in my family have a very shallow notch where the cruciate ligaments rest, so they pop out and tear easily. All my boys have torn at least one cruciate ligament. This son has been skiing since he was seven, a strong skier. The accident happened when he abruptly veered away from an out-of-control ski boarder on the Australian snowfields. When hereditary factors are involved there is little one can do. Karma!

In 1993 I go through a painful ACL operation. I have many more enjoyable years of skiing, although I also have another two operations, both meniscus repairs.

My happiest skiing was in the USA in the mid to late 1990s. Steamboat Springs was my favourite resort. The feeling of exhilaration was unbelievable as I skied between the trees. You do not have to be an expert to do that, just have a steady tempo and good rhythm. The sensation of going amongst the trees in the crisp morning air is indescribable. Skiing gave me the joy of using my body. It was worth the pain from all the falls, the naked fear when you find that you have accidentally gone into a difficult black run and wonder whether you will ever get out!

It was at Steamboat Springs that I had my most thrilling skiing day. We had joined a group known as the "Over The Hill Gang". The group consisted of older, experienced skiers, who would show visitors the different runs in the resort. We did the morning runs with them, at lunchtime meeting up with their friends, the skiing instructors.

One day I left lunch at the same time as one of the instructors, who was on his own. I thought it would be a fantastic experience to follow him down! The snow was good and the run not crowded. I followed his turns and curves, having the most wonderful long ski run. He got to the bottom and I stopped just behind him. He turned around and faced me. "Are you the skier who followed me all the way down?" I timidly admitted it. He smiled at me and said "You are a very good skier."

I could not believe my ears. Would Kit believe me when I told him this ? I knew I skied well that morning, probably my best ever! I had received compliments before. Covered in my ski gear no one knew that I was middle-aged. The scars on my face and damage to my body did not matter. I just wanted to do well and get Kit to be proud of me. Of course, I enjoyed the sport too. The words of the instructor made my trip worthwhile.

It left me smiling each of the remaining days of the ski holiday. I still smile as I recall that scene so many years later!

After a few years, our favourite ski resort is Lake Tahoe in Nevada, where the runs cater for all levels. We also find good skiing friends, Ted and Al. Now we not only enjoy the skiing but friendship as well. We are lucky people! Kit and Al form a gambling partnership, while Ted contributes to the capital. It is a successful collaboration and we earn our dinner at the casino after the day's skiing.

We go to Las Vegas after leaving Lake Tahoe. We had been there in 1976, but only for an overnight visit. We are keen on the shows at the beginning, but soon the gambling is getting equal attention. We have acquired a new vice.

Both Kit and I, as we used to say, are not goody goodies, and the Chinese are said to be natural gamblers. Kit played poker for money while still a student at the university. I was not a novice either. As a young child I had watched the workers play "Three cards", a simple gambling game, during the Chinese New Year. The shops were closed for three days each year, and gambling was how the workers spent their time. They had received their annual bonuses and were flush with funds. It did not take me long to know the game and I witnessed the excitement of the workers, their sweating and shouts, as they played. Hilda had taught and subsidised us to gamble at card games later on. I could play Mah-jong at ten years of age and taught Kit to play the game. Before long, his natural talent took him past my level of expertise.

In Las Vegas I take to the slot machines while Kit loves playing blackjack.

20 The good years

I had watched Kit chasing golf balls since 1964. I had no interest in the game but was pleased that he got his regular exercise and relaxation. In Ipoh he would spend not only the weekends, but any odd free afternoon at the golf club as long as there was daylight left to see the ball. I would take the two boys to the club for the curry puffs and potato chips, treats that they loved. My usual joke was that it was to let them see their father so they could remember what he looked like!

I went for a couple of golf lessons just to see what it was like. I did not relate to the game, unlike skiing, which appealed to me from the start.

Kit continues to be fascinated by golf in our new life in Sydney. He introduces our second son to the game, gaining a regular partner and fellow golf nut. We also have a good social life. We are out at dinners with other migrants, our Aussie friends and Kit's colleagues from the hospitals. Kit is a good mixer and loves company.

At one dinner I meet Yin, a seemingly quiet and soft-spoken lady. We find we have a common interest in fruit. Yin tells me of the wholesale fruit markets around Sydney. We can buy boxes of fruit and share it, which means we can indulge the range of delicious fruit grown in Australia! Yin only lives on the next street. And the other big discovery is that she is a golfing wife. She encourages me to take up the game and invites me to play at her club.

In Kuala Lumpur I most often socialise with my sisters and do not mix a lot. As a result, I can be gullible, thinking everyone is well-intentioned and genuine. I do not realise how lucky I have been with my friends in Sixth Form and at university. Shortly after joining the ladies' section at Kit's golf club I receive a call from another golfing wife and meet a delightful lady with a honeyed tongue. In hindsight I see how easily I am carried away by flattery. I think I have found a friend for life! We enjoy ourselves on the course. I think air swings are great fun! My new friend takes lessons every day – no more air swings for her. She develops a beautiful action and I find she has moved on to join the better players without telling me. On the golf course you learn more than just golf.

Yet I am not blind to the fact that I am unlikely to excel in the game. At best I may become a mediocre player. With an anterior cruciate ligament injury on the left leg, a ligament tear on the right, the inability to swing well, plus small weak hands, what chance do I have with a game that demands so much of the human body? On top of everything else, I am no young athlete. With skiing I have the balance and graceful movement required. I love skiing, I do not love golf. At the same time, now that I am playing it, I want to do well because it is a game Kit loves.

I approach Kit to let me go for lessons. Lessons are expensive. Kit believes in working on the game, especially the short game. He reminds me that he got me skiing, so he will get me golfing, but underestimates the difficulty of golf for the older person.

I am frustrated by golf, and unrealistically wait for the breakthrough that does not come. However, I do get a good result occasionally. My target is to get my ball nearest to the pin on the shortest hole on the course. Joy, oh joy! I succeed and bring home a large box of chocolates from the ladies' Christmas competition.

I serve two years on the ladies committee, but my contribution is limited as I have neither proficient nor experienced in playing golf. It is the social aspect to which I contribute. I am proud of the sketches I produce at our annual ladies' concerts. My area of expertise is knowledge of China and South East Asia. I want the Aussie lady golfers to know something about the Chinese, and my imagination helps. The exotic Chinese costumes will surely capture the ladies' attention, and I decide to work on that.

But before the glitter and the glamour of sequinned and beaded garments, I want the Aussie ladies to know how and when the Chinese came to this country. The first Chinese came in 1847 to work as shepherds. In 1856 they came in their hundreds, then thousands, for the gold rush. The first large group landed at Guichen Bay, near Robe in South Australia, because they could not pay the ten pound fee imposed on Chinese migrants by the Victorian government. Instead, they walked over 400 kilometres to the gold fields of Ballarat and Bendigo, each dressed in the loose Chinese tunic with its high collar, black trousers and black cloth shoes, balancing two cloth bundles, one on each end of a wooden pole. The small bundles represented all their material possessions.

Chinese arrivals walking to the Victorian gold fields by SC Brees c. 1856. Courtesy of the State Library Victoria

Each man had his black hair neatly plaited into a pigtail hanging down his back. Perhaps it was this scene that brought the first outburst of "you Chinese all look the same" from a bystander. Chinese migration to Australia almost disappeared completely because of the White Australia Policy, which was in force from 1901 to 1966.

This was the opening scene of my first concert sketch: I was dressed as a Chinese coolie walking across the stage with my wooden pole and worldly belongings. I was also the compère. Then I introduced my three beautiful Chinese ladies, all dressed up. They wore traditional two-piece Chinese wedding dresses – a long sleeved blouse and a floor-length skirt, one bright red, one black and another green, all heavily embroidered. The black one had the more elaborate pattern with "waves of eternity", normally associated with Chinese royalty, at the bottom of the skirt. The red dress had a dragon and a phoenix, while the green dress displayed the Chinese peony and peach blossom. Then entered the other Chinese members in the short cheongsam and the long evening cheongsam. It must have been the first time our golf club had seen such a display of Chinese costumes. Unfortunately, the concert was not for men's eyes, as it was a ladies only event. The sketch was a hit, especially with the older lady golfers.

Li and her golf club revue cast

Another year we exhibited the Chinese sword dance, gracefully done by two Chinese members. We gave a simple kung fu demonstration with kung fu costumes. We had a scene of Chinese children at play, showing simple clothes and toys, as well as Chinese lanterns, cymbals, gongs, bells and a flute. For our final year we included a touch of South East Asia. The theme given to us was the nine o'clock news, and I dressed up my cast as newsreaders in national costumes from Malaysia, Vietnam, Korea, Japan and China.

That was our last sketch. I hear that there are no annual concerts these days.

The glitter and glamour were fun to behold, although there was one unexpected reaction beforehand. When I told Yin of my desire to bring some knowledge of Chinese culture to our Aussie golfers I was shocked by her reply. Firstly, I discovered that she was afraid I would make myself more popular than her. Secondly, she thought poorly of us migrants.

Yin did not mince her words with me. She warned me not to try to contribute anything to the concert, because we would be so inferior in our language and delivery skills compared to the local Australian women. She emphasised that I would fall flat on my face, die of embarrassment and be an abysmal failure. That I should thank her for her timely warning. Yet Yin and my other golfing friend were most keen to appear on the stage in the attractive costumes when I proved her wrong!

Yin also told me that it is only the game that matters in a golf club, and the fastest way to gain acceptance is to show excellence in the game. I noted that there were some who viewed me with suspicion. Nonetheless, I dug deeper and found a wealth of friendships amongst the ladies. There was kind, gentle Ruth, supportive and willing to give everyone a chance. Others like Eileen, always fair and rational. There were other migrants, Phaik and Cherry. What more can one ask for?

Fellow migrants should be aware that sometimes your own kind may not wish you well for various reasons. Do not be discouraged. Your fluency in the language may not be the best, but your imagination and capacity for hard work will not necessarily be poorer than that of others.

*

It is 1992 and we relocate again. The three older children are working and have moved out, while the youngest has gone to live near his university, so there are only the two of us left. Kit and I think it would be lovely to wake to birdsong and look out to the trees and bushes. We select Beecroft, and Kit finds an old two bedroom house that opens onto a beautiful wide road lined with jacaranda trees. It is a purple fairyland when the trees are in bloom.

The house is very old and needs extensive renovations. I am hesitant, but Kit loves the place. We make a terrible blunder. We should have demolished the whole place and rebuilt. Our biggest mistake is not to increase the number of bedrooms by at least one. But the first problem is a big tree stump in the front garden: heavy equipment has to be brought in to remove it. We have a good builder, but unforeseen costs start creeping in, such as to remove a termite nest in the back garden and other minor but expensive issues.

Kit and I move into our beautiful home. Our bedroom looks into the bush below. The Gang Gang cockatoos and the King parrots visit our garden. They are the less common birds and are gorgeous.

Male Gang Gang cockatoo

The mornings are beautiful. Our sitting room has 180° views across the bushland, and we have full length windows. The curtains cost a small fortune, but the room is perfect for entertaining. I have also splurged on a large oval rosewood dining table with matching chairs. To complement it I have purchased two large mother of pearl portraits of classical Chinese beauties, which I hang on the dining room wall. I have a huge kitchen and Kit has a large wine cellar. It is relaxing to sit outside on the balcony at sunset, although we do not have enough evenings free to do that often enough. We are proud of the house and invite guests there for pre-dinner drinks before the wedding of our second son.

When winter comes I discover that the downstairs rooms get very damp and mouldy. And insects swarm inside. Every winter's day I have to sweep out a certain tiny insect by the dozens! But Kit likes the house, and we stay until 1999.

While living there we learn to appreciate opera. We start to visit our beautiful Sydney Opera House with its unique architecture. We pay two hundred dollars for tickets to a performance by Luciano Pavarotti. Of course, we find ourselves so far away we can only see his face on the side video screens.

In the mid-nineties we watch and enjoy opera on TV. My greatest thrill is listening to Pavarotti singing Nessun Dorma in Turandot. I still get goosebumps listening to it. My other favourite singer is Plácido Domingo. Which woman would not enjoy watching him and his dreamy eyes as he sings La Paloma? Then comes José Carreras and all of them together as The Three Tenors.

It is such a treat to watch The Three Tenors and witness the rivalry between Domingo and Pavarotti. How to describe my enjoyment of their rendition of O sole mio? One cannot but be aware of the excitement of Zubin Mehta as he jumps up and down conducting the concert! I doubt that this would have been on TV in Malaysia and enjoy what the western world offers me. Life is good for me and Kit.

Harbin, 1993

It is 1993. I have finished my master's degree and decide to stop going to university. I had promised myself that I would spend more time with Kit, which is why I had taken up golf. Kit and I continue skiing, as we both love it. Life is not boring. Grace makes her regular forays and each time she appears Kit and I have our fights.

My second son is posted to China by the US company he works for. He rings and offers me a holiday, as I am recuperating from my anterior cruciate ligament operation. I am only too glad to visit China again. I must admit that my language skills are gone. How could I have let this occur? It just happened as I turned to other things.

It has been eight years since I was last in China. The place I most want to see is the city of Harbin. Harbin has been at the back of my mind ever since I found out about Japanese Army Unit 731 and its base there, where they experimented on live people during World War II. I read that the biological and chemical experiments were done in near secrecy. The US Government knew afterwards, but did not publicise the experiments, as the Japanese had willingly shared the results with them after the war!

I fly into Beijing. My son has a two bedroom apartment rented by his company in an expensive part of Beijing. He is busy with work and has little time to spare. I am only too delighted to wander around by myself, happy with my own company. He has a girl pursuing him. She waits outside his unit every day until he comes back from work. His hours are uncertain, and she waits for long periods of time. He does not seem to be smitten by her, but I tell him to treat her better! She offers to accompany me around the sights, and once we go to the Imperial Palace together.

Through a travel agent in Beijing I book a hotel room in a respectable area of Harbin. I fly there and have trouble sleeping, as the sun does not seem to set. I have difficulty finding the experimental station. My enquiries are met with negative answers, but I am not going to give up and finally find the place. I expect a large memorial hall, but find a primary school. In a corner I find a small exhibition room with lots of written material, mostly in Chinese, with little in English. I see photographs of dead bodies and notes on death brought about by the various diseases: plague, dysentery, typhus, poison gas, frostbite, etc. There must have been details on what was injected or how the victims were exposed. And there were glass tanks with actual bodies preserved in chemical solutions.

The forerunner of Japanese Kwantung Army Unit 731 was a chemical and germ warfare army unit founded in Harbin in 1932.

In 1936 the experimental station was moved to the place known as Pingfang, 20 kilometres south of Harbin. Between 1933 to 1945 at least 3,000 people were reported to have become victims of Unit 731, including Russians and Mongolians. Who knows what the true figures were? All the main structures and facilities were demolished before the Japanese surrendered. There was little left for me or anyone else to see.

I went to Harbin because I wanted to find answers. Why were these people killed? It was neither a cheap trip nor a pleasure trip.

We talk of people daring to dream, aspiring to greater heights, but had these victims the time to even think? Food, survival, what else could they concentrate on? The physical pain and mental anguish from being experimented upon. Somebody made the decisions. Was it the Japanese Militarists again? Why were you so cruel to the Chinese and others? You have such a close history with the Chinese. You learn so much from them. Your military leaders chose to turn your beautiful youth into killing machines devoid of feelings. Your soldiers chose to throw babies into the air and bayonet them as they fell downwards. A mountain of dead bodies was left in Nanjing. Human remains were strewn along your path as your soldiers burst through south east Asia. Was it the madness of war?

I wonder if the Japanese militarist war cabinet sent their own sons to battle. They deployed youths whose courage and dedication were second to none. Young men who were taught that to sacrifice themselves was the greatest good they could do for their country. I weep for those who never saw action in war because they died on their bunks, dreams unfulfilled, when their ships sank. Yet they would have caused so much death and destruction had they succeeded. We see the dark side of man. Man's inhumanity to man.

These are but the thoughts of a person who loves her fellow people.

I have more than a day left in Harbin. I visit the sites, walking along Heilongjiang (Black Dragon River), visiting the area bordering Russia, seeing the onion-domed buildings there. I say goodbye, for I will never visit again, and fly back to Beijing.

I willingly revisit the Imperial Palace, a place no longer forbidden! My son takes me to the Great Wall. I last visited in 1986, when it was winter and I had been too ill to climb. This time it is warm and I run up as far as my recuperating left leg allows. I feel the rough bricks, hoping to touch the ancient parts of the wall. Doing that seems to give me joy.

Through the mists of time I recall a strange experience from that visit to Beijing. I meet a person selling cloisonné Christmas decorations. He is tall, in his fifties. We haggle over the price. I stand firm, as I had checked out prices the day before. My bargaining skills acquired in Malaysia are still good and get a very good bargain. He smiles. It is a beautiful smile. He congratulates me and taps me on my shoulder. Normally, I would immediately move away and react angrily to being touched. But I have a sudden sensation that I have known this person before! I am stunned and puzzled for the next half an hour! I push the thought aside. Kit says I have an over-active imagination.

I return to Sydney, having had a good short holiday.

India, Nepal and Thailand

It is December 1993 and I am still recovering from my anterior cruciate operation. No skiing, but I am active and moving around. I encourage Kit to try a guided tour; we decide to see India. We seize upon the first one available, which turns out to be a budget tour. We would prefer a bit more luxury, but those are scheduled for the months we do not wish to be away.

We see the usual sights in India, but the hotels are not what we wish for. We do not mind the age, but the cleanliness is lacking. At one hotel I ask Kit whether he has been cutting his nails. He gives me a quizzical look and replies that he has not yet found the time. I decide to opt for discretion and not poke my nose into obscure corners! Fortunately, there is plenty of hot water.

The sights are wonderful. The Taj Mahal lives up to expectations. The recommendation is to see it at night, the best view being under the moonlight. Unfortunately the place is closed at night, no visitors allowed! We visit Delhi, Jodhpur, Jaipur, Agra and Varanasi. The cities, the fortresses, all stand out as historical sites, but there is so much dust, dirt and poverty. I see teeming humanity and disease on the streets.

At Varanasi, the crowds come to bathe and cleanse themselves in the Holy Ganges. In the distance a cremation takes place on the water, while nearby floats a dead dog.

We make our own light moments. As always in group tours, one finds companions who are compatible and fun to be with. One evening we are with two other such couples, returning to the hotel by trishaw. Kit suggests a race back and the young riders agree. We thought we would add more fun, so we start bribing the riders to speed up. The other two couples catch on and soon we are racing along the streets of

Delhi, the wives screeching with laughter. I think we were first, only by a little, largely because we bribed the most!

A second incident is a painful memory. My youngest son had presented me with a bag of sweet corn before we left Sydney. I am an incorrigible muncher. Yes, I break a molar, leaving a sharp edge cutting into the inside of my cheek. All I want is to get it rounded off, the rest of the job to be left for my dentist back in Sydney. Kit and I set off in the morning to look for a dentist. We find a street dentist who understands some English. We manage to tell him what we want. He does an adequate job. I test it and am satisfied. Kit reaches for his wallet but we are surprised. The dentist refuses payment, saying we are guests in India. We press him but he stands firm. He could have made a killing, for we would have paid him handsomely. I remember you, my humble dentist, for the rest of my life, and gladly relate our story.

The sights we capture on our cameras, but the human incidents we capture in our hearts. There are also amusing and unusual incidents to recall. Our tour guide is not impressive, but he tries his best. His very heavy accent is a handicap, making his comments sound more like Hindi than English. The monotone does not help. My group mates have confused looks. I try my best to recall the Indian history I learnt and start to do some explaining. Soon my companions turn to me for help. Our guide does not seem offended. I see him moving to the corner and closing his eyes. Is he able to sleep standing? Does he have a second job and a large family?

Our itinerary includes a visit to a school. It is morning assembly. Out steps a smart-looking girl of about twelve who leads the assembly. She has two thickish plaits, neatly done. I stand behind her as an honoured guest. We each contribute a small sum to the school. From my position I can see the back of her head clearly. There are nits dancing in and out of her plaits. I am reminded how common nits are, even though they are easy to get rid of with modern treatments.

Next day we have one of our highlights, and visit the Ranthambore Game Park. We are also subject to their "games". A tiger has been sighted and fresh footprints found on the muddy ground. We are driven around in an open long jeep, cautioned to keep very quiet. It all ends two hours later. We are told we have been unlucky, as the tiger must have gone into hiding. A day later we get to ride an elephant and a camel. So now I have ridden a donkey and camel in Egypt and an elephant and a camel in India!

*

Nepal was an option we had added to the India trip. We were going so close to this mysterious kingdom we might as well see it. It is a once in a lifetime visit.

Nepal, a small remote kingdom, yet not that remote to me. It is the motherland of my primary school classmate, little Lily Naidoo. We were fellow victims of an ignorant teacher who did not understand that our Asian culture did not encourage us to answer questions in class, although Lily suffered more than I did. I learned to speak up, she did not. Lily had long plaits, which the teacher would pull as she screamed at us. We were terrified of her!

Nepal had been a land of professional soldiers. The British in India had discovered their prowess in fighting and had recruited the Nepalese into the British Army. The Nepalese followed the British to Malaya and that was how I met Lily.

In 1993 Nepal is a small and poor country ruled by a royal family. It is no longer a true despotic regime, as reforms are taking place and there are demands for still greater freedoms. Sightseeing in Kathmandu does not take too much time because of its size. The city is very polluted because of the new factories.

The highlight of the tour is to be a trip up the mountain to a hill resort, from where one can catch sight of Mount Everest. There we are, with a whole bunch of other tourists, seated before sunrise, waiting for the first rays of sunshine to hit

Mount Everest. Unfortunately, it is a cloudy day, so there is no glimpse of the famed mountain! Instead a disgusting sight greets us. Here on the mountainside are aging European males fondling young Nepalese boys. Pederasts. They are also on holiday.

The boys avert their eyes as we pass them. The indecencies that poverty forces on the young! We are driven back to the city and flown out early the next day.

It is a happier sight that greets us as the plane approaches Bangkok. The temples glittering in the morning light are as dazzling as ever. It is Kit's first visit, while I was here thirty four years ago, a young, keen student looking forward to the challenges of life. Our group does the rounds of the sights. The perceptive guide can see we are tired and finds us a good massage place. We wives are placed on beds next to our husbands, but that does not stop the suggestive sighs they are making, the guys trying to outdo each other. However, I must admit that the two hour massage was one of the best I have ever had. These Thai girls have such strong hands and make clever use of them. That evening we are taken to a Thai banquet with good Thai food. For me there is the extra treat – Thai dancing. When the Ramvong begins I cannot resist going down to dance. I learnt the dance as a child in Malaya, as Thai dance troupes often visited. The Thai stopover was a pleasing end to the holiday.

21 My cup runneth over, 1999 - 2000

Our Beecroft bush view home had been Kit's choice, and we've been there for seven years. We are getting tired of it and wish to be nearer the city. The mosquitoes in the back garden feast on me on laundry days, other little flying insects keep me busy sweeping out the downstairs rooms, and wiping off the mould is doing my back no good.

In late 1998 a friend takes me to see a new housing development that is a little more upmarket than our current suburb, very attractive and next to the Parramatta River. He and his wife are totally charmed by it, and have placed a deposit on one of the new homes. They had debated about letting others know, as the husband is the quiet sort and wants a peaceful life. I am lucky he decides to show me the place. There is no harm in going for a "look see" and it ends with me finding my dream home!

The particular house I wanted had already been snapped up, having what I thought was the best view of the water, but I have a serious talk to Kit. I take him to see the new development and he catches my excitement.

We are seriously considering one of the houses, but while we are in the sales office looking at the plans for the area Kit spots it: number 19, my house! Whoever had originally put a deposit on the place had released it. The house is still under construction and expected to be completed in another nine months. All three bedrooms are upstairs, while most of the other homes have a bedroom downstairs. At this point in time Kit has no problems with his legs. He also never entertains the thought that his mother would want to move in, as she tried to do after her partner died, shortly before we moved from Beecroft!

We sit down and do our sums. Yes, says Kit, we can raise the money. We sign a contract for the new house and pay the

10% deposit. My job now is to get our current place ready for sale.

It takes us many months to sell the house. I am no novice, and on viewing days put in my best effort, creating flower and fruit arrangements. The crochet pieces and tablecloths made by sister Mei are attractive. She won many competitions with her crochet work. The silk and embroidered decorative pieces I bought on my visits to China are all over the house. Our real estate agent warns me to beware of thefts, especially of small decorative items. Children who accompany their parents can be a source of danger. I learn something new! There are so many comments on how lovely the place looks, but it does not hide the fact that the house has only two bedrooms.

The house is finally sold, but the process has been exhausting and disappointing. The amount we receive does not cover our purchase price and renovations. Kit takes it well, saying "You win some, you lose some." And it was not a complete loss, as we had enjoyed the house.

My disappointment is pushed aside by the excitement of moving. I am caught up with furnishing and decorating the new house. We spend more than we ever had on doing up a new home, but we have to do it justice! It is a happy time, and I go to bed exhausted every night. Gushing with excitement, I write to sister-in-law Chun about my dream home. Her reply is a dampener. She tells me to watch out, as I am living beyond our means. We have worked hard and put all our savings into this beautiful home. We sell all our other investments and raise enough funds for the home without borrowing from the bank. I wish she could have been pleased for us.

In September we move in. The internal stairs are only a short flight and the staircase is wide. The master bedroom has a walk-in wardrobe and a big bathroom at one end. At the other end it opens into a large balcony. The balcony and second bedroom look out to a walkway and the water beyond. It is a splendid view and these homes will never be built out.

A nearby view of the Parramatta River

The second bedroom will be our guest room. As guests are infrequent, it means we will enjoy much privacy. The third bedroom is at the back, and we plan to make it into our study. It faces the amenities area, looking over the two swimming pools and the gym. Within the house itself there is so much space – an extra-large kitchen and sitting room. Some years later our first granddaughter stood on my feet while I waltzed us around that sitting room to her squeals of laughter.

Kit and I are thrilled with the arrival of that granddaughter in 1999. We refer to each other as grandpa and grandma for a month before we revert back to our usual names. With our shared sense of good humour there is much laughter in the home. I start to look after the baby when she is six weeks old. Our daughter drops her over three days a week, and I spend two days on the golf course. I now have the time I'd never had for my own children, and discover that a child can bring so much joy!

At the same time, a new fear emerges. For many years I had lived in fear that Kit would leave me. In our early years of marriage Grace had told me that she could make him do that, for she came first in his heart. (When we were in our seventies, Kit told me that he had never thought of leaving me. I was also in my seventies when I first went to see a psychologist to learn I have depression.) Now, I become obsessed with the risk of dropping the baby. My fear is no better with the second grandchild.

One evening in late 1999, as Kit muses over his glass of red wine, he pronounces that it has been a good year for us. He seems to have pushed aside the memory of Grace's dramatic attempt to move in. The two major events that followed, the welcome birth of our beautiful first grandchild in August, and moving into my dream home in September, dominated everything else.

*

However, the year 2000 has to be the happiest year of my life. We continue with our skiing and golfing activities. We have wonderful skiing companions, Tet and Alfred. Kit and I are indeed fortunate to be blessed with these friends. Each trip with them is enjoyable. In 2000 we ski at Heavenly in the USA. On the golf front we are also lucky. We have found another couple whose company we enjoy. Cee is a lovely person and has a husband to match. We seem to be laughing a lot together and celebrate New Year's Eve with them, watching the fireworks over the Sydney Harbour Bridge from their unit in North Sydney. We toast in the new year. We travel to Queensland for a golfing week each year. I have my good friends at the golf club, gentle kind Ruth and Eileen, although I still rail at my golf instead of spending time on improvement.

In June, Kit and my daughter plan a surprise for me – a 60th birthday dinner party with all my golfing mates at our club. Ruth and Cee make speeches and say nice things about me. I feel shy but pleased. It is a wonderful party!

Then one fine Sunday in September, in a club competition, my golf ball crosses the pond, lands short of the pin and rolls into the hole! I am delighted I am playing with Kit, and he witnesses it all. The other couple, strangers, witness their first hole-in-one and congratulate me. Of course, Kit treats them to drinks. I can proudly say it was a straight ball, a decent hit. Of course, one has to be lucky as well!

Our little granddaughter turns one. She races to me each time she spots me and is such a happy child. Her laughter rings through the house. Kit is also getting much joy playing with her and sweeps her up each time she runs to him. She trails behind him when he returns home from work, and I have to tell her "You cannot follow Grandpa into the shower, he needs a good wash after a day's work", but she is not convinced. After dinner Kit drives her home.

My good year seems to roll on into 2001. Our second grandchild makes her appearance in May. Another beautiful child with skin even paler than her sister's. Their father is of Irish descent, straightforward in character and easy to get along with. There is no pretence, no tricks about him. He is fair and honest in judgement. I enjoy his sense of humour and am relaxed in his company.

Our second granddaughter gives me one of those unforgettable moments in life. She is three years old and we are playing together. I place her little feet on mine and waltz her around the sitting room of my dream home, as I had done with her older sister. As expected, she giggles with joy as I move faster and faster round the room. A spontaneous outburst from her – "I love you, Grandma!"

I am stunned and time-travel back to 1943, to another 3 year old who had so much love to give, but no one to give it to …

I ponder over my granddaughters. They are the future of Australia, their home, and I think that they will never emigrate for political reasons. My prayers are for Australia to have good leaders who will serve and guide all the population and never have cause to drive them away. There should be no more reluctant migrants!

22 Other endings

Inevitably, many main characters who figured in my life have passed on. Kit and I both lost our mothers in 2009: Luk May died in Kuala Lumpur, Grace in a nursing home in Singapore.

My sister-in-law Chun passed away in 2014.

Kit retired from the work he loved in 2011, forced to do so because of neurological problems. His weakening legs were causing too many falls. He fell particularly badly in 2015, suffering a brain haemorrhage, losing part of his memory and the ability to walk. Life continued for him, but from a wheelchair. He passed away in 2020, when one of his lungs collapsed and he died from aspiration pneumonia.

23 Have I come full circle?

2022. A bit more, a bit further, I must go further. A silver haired lady tells herself she must walk on. She needs the exercise, she needs to get back into life, for her time has not yet come, although she wants to go. She pushes herself along the foreshore walk in Concord, Sydney. Her legs can still carry her, although she suffers from occasional giddy spells.

1943. A three year old girl walks alongside the wall of a shophouse on sturdy little legs. It is Kuala Lumpur, Malaya. She does not know why, but there is a compulsion to keep walking. She does not understand, she has no context, but there is a feeling of sadness and loneliness.

Back to Sydney, the 81 year old has the same feeling of sadness and loneliness.

Has life come full circle? It is the same person. At the beginning, just before she is able to reason logically, and near the end, her mind filled with a lifetime of thoughts and memories. At three years of age and at 81 years of age. Yet was it that long ago? It seems like yesterday …

The scene in early 2022 was when I came out of a haze of sorrow following 15 months of deep mourning for Kit.

I am sure that three year olds can feel sadness and loneliness, because those were amongst the earliest feelings I remember. I just wanted to explain.

Music in the night

Another day I awoke to two tunes that continued to play in my head as I walked along the foreshore of the Parramatta River: Tao Hua Bu Zhang Kai (Peach blossoms do not stay open for long), and Yueh Lai Xi'ang (The fragrance comes only at night).

These Chinese songs were famous when I was growing up. I can only recall parts of the first song, even less of the second. There are so many songs of which I remember only fragments.

Remembering these particular songs, I think I now understand my attachment, my feelings, for the country loved by Zhang Yu, MahMah, Ah Chieh and my parents.

Ah Chieh taught me songs in Mandarin that I learnt by heart, rote learning. I can still repeat them, although I do not know what they mean, and I remember the music, the haunting tunes. It is the sad music that tugs at my heartstrings. Songs, stories and movies about China are all sad. They appeal to the sadness within me.

I absorbed the longing for China from my elders, what is now called cultural bereavement. I also never lost that sadness from my early years, from the neglect, the canings, the insults hurled at me. That is why I feel I am different from my siblings, except, perhaps, brother Yeh.

One song I remember often was sung by Bai Kwong. It was about a destitute young girl who ended up as a prostitute on the streets of Shanghai. Another song was about the moon shining on a desolate road in a deserted village. It was wartime. Yet another was Wan Li Zhang Cheng, The Great Wall of China. I sing the words, but do not understand them. I only know it is sad.

From Ah Chieh I picked up some Mandarin words, so I did understand a bit as a child, but too little. These songs and the music appealed to the growing Li, a sensitive, sentimental individual. These tunes returned repeatedly to little Li at night. When she could not sleep, the haunting tunes seemed to call out to her from somewhere. It is these melodies that chained and claimed me as I grew. Invisible unbreakable chains. Sentimental, illogical, but they have haunted me for a lifetime. I finally understand ...

I understand, too, why I so easily fell for the Chinese films on TV. They gave me much-needed distraction from my grieving for Kit. I had wept silently day and night for 15 months after his departure. Then, one day, I had by chance turned on the Chinese movie channel instead of the news channel I habitually watched. I had only wanted to know what was happening around me in my country, Australia. Now I watched the costume dramas of ancient China, moving on to films on the Second World War and civil wars. I found them interesting. They helped me mend and learn to accept life without Kit. I am still learning ...

A final word

I have lived and travelled the road of life for a long time. I believe I have learnt some valuable lessons in life. I do not want to harbour grudges, nor do l want to allow hatred to dwell within me. One needs to let go, yet that is difficult. Only by allowing love to govern us are we able to find peace, to look forward to reuniting with loved ones long gone, and leave this world willingly. In this way, I have indeed been fortunate, finding peace these last few years, although perhaps not entirely deserving of it.

Each individual views life through her own eyes, perhaps through coloured lenses.

In a world in transition Grace chose traditional values, for that best served her interest. Li preferred her modern world of western learning, even if unable to avoid certain traditions. She clung stubbornly to what she felt were her inalienable rights as an individual.

Li was also over-romantic and overly sentimental. She was a dreamer, oftentimes neither sensible nor practical. Perhaps she wanted too much to make up for what she had missed as a child. However, there were also many times when she was able to size up situations and be realistic. Perhaps, after all, Li was an ordinary person who felt and experienced much.

*

A final poem with which to end the story of little Li, and the 82 year old adult Li as she writes this book:

Life

I have lived thro'
life with the shadow,
I have lived thro'
life with a husband
I do not fully understand
Yet I have clung to.
I have lived thro' pain and sorrow
Yet now I learn it is simply called life.
Life has given me so much.
I have learnt joy,
I have learnt conflict and mental anguish,
I have finally learnt acceptance.
I know others have suffered much, much more,
But I can only write of what I know and experienced.
I know of my own despair,
When I do not wish to live anymore.
When I feel I am bereft of love.
I have survived
As the rosebush survived.
In my eighty first year I find I am able
To accept what I have known
But refused to admit all these years.
I am not Fortune's favourite,
Neither am I her outcast.
In my old age I am lonely,
Sometimes sad.

But I have peace,
I sleep well, I am no longer in pain.
I also wish
For reunion with loved ones long gone.
I wish my remaining loved ones
Peace and happiness in this life.
I wish the best for
My fellow men who are still
On their journey through life.
I leave my blessings while
I await my turn
To leave …

Epilogue

It has been a long journey, but I am no longer troubled by or relive the conflicts in so much of my life. I have experienced joy and love, as well as pain and sorrow on this long trip.

In writing my book I journeyed back through time. I went through the piles of letters that Kit and I wrote each other through our courtship days, plus during the years of separation when he was in Australia and New Zealand and I was in England and China. They were not sloppy sentimental letters, but rather accounts of what was happening around us. I was also an incorrigible note-maker, and would write whenever I was sad. With my strong memory and vivid recall, reading those letters made me again feel the pain of the difficult times in the past. But this time I gained insights into life. It is my hope that my writings will help others to gain their own insights.

I do not have the answers to life. They do not matter anymore, for they are not needed when we leave this life. It is an imperfect world. We are imperfect. We do not carry our petty triumphs with us from this world.

I thank Kit for the life he gave me. He lived long, but his last 15 years was a journey of suffering. He was the Confucian gentleman, always there to help and to give of himself. Yet now, on reflection, I do not think we should have been partners in life. We were never able to talk about things that bothered me – mostly the way his mother treated me when she and I were alone. Kit abhorred conflict and confrontation. He avoided conversation with me, probably for fear that the subject of his mother would be brought up. Perhaps he saw the unrelenting stubbornness in me. Perhaps he considered it was a hopeless task. I felt that, with his nature Kit, could have married any woman and created a happy marriage. He could have given his mother what she wanted in a daughter-in-law and there would have been happiness for both mother and son.

And as for me, I am sure I could have made a successful life for myself, alone or with another. Grace cost me too much pain, but convinced me for so long that I was to blame for our conflicts.

I had been a hopeless sentimentalist, clinging to the belief of Ah Heng, the housekeeper from my childhood, in the Chinese saying that a person's life consists of two halves. If you experience pain and distress in the first half of your life then your second half will be filled with happiness.

Now I know I did not deserve those years of torment during my married life, worse than my emotionally deprived and physically abusive childhood.

*

What about my mental problems? I am thankful I can understand something of them at last. Unable to hurt those who hurt me, not wanting to hurt others, but discovering the power to hurt someone – myself. I call it the wish to self-destruct.

This desire to self-destruct does not disappear, even with some understanding of it. It is still there but I keep it under control. I do not go to tall buildings from which one can jump, I do not walk close to the riverbank or expose myself to sharp and dangerous instruments. I rationalise that harming myself will only harm my loved ones, and they do not deserve to be punished!

When you think that you are worthy of love and someone loves you, the negative thoughts are suppressed.

*

My story also has a message for Australians. There needs to be patience with migrants, for many of us carry heavy baggage. Some of us are damaged. The young ones will recover. The hope is in the next generation.

Kit and I were born and spent our youth in a beautiful country that unfortunately failed us and made us migrants who sought and found a new home in Australia.

Kit never had divided loyalties. Australia gave him and his family a home. He was a proud Australian. My children know no other home, although they were born elsewhere. They grew up loving this country. For my beautiful grandchildren Australia is HOME and LOVE.

As for me, Australia is home and love, and there is also love of others. Love is always good. However little Li is a breed from the past. To her the adult migrants passed on their love for the sad, war-wearied and poverty-stricken country from whence they came, reluctant migrants. But China is now rich and powerful.

However, China cannot expect unconditional love from generations descended from the original diaspora.

The children of reluctant migrants love their new homes and so they should. They can have affection for the country of their ancestors, but their duty and love is due to their new country. So, too, should the new country honour and respect them. No more discrimination, but live as members of one national family.

*

There are others like me, but we will be gone soon. I have extended family in China, maybe dozens I have not met and do not know of. My wish is that the youth of Australia never fight the youth of China.

I am tired. I am at my journey's end. I wish to see my loved ones from long ago …

Acknowledgements

To my editor and friend I owe a debt of gratitude. My friend Anne Ying and her husband brought you to see me. I said that I had a story which needed to be told. As I started to relate it I began to cry and could not stop the flow of tears. It was a catharsis. As you said, I owed it to myself to let it all out. I am so glad you decided to help me, that this weird old lady did not turn you off.

I had just begun to "wake" from my grieving for Kit, to walk along the foreshore and enjoy the beauty around me. With your encouragement I became bolder and more confident in my writing. You helped me bring out what sat within me for so long.

My two granddaughters gave me their support and encouragement. My younger granddaughter was always there for me. My older granddaughter was important at a crucial time when I felt there was too much sadness and I did not want to continue writing. She told me not to give up. This was before I met Dinah.

I quote from my final poem: "I am not Fortune's favourite, neither am I her outcast." I have a choice in life. I chose to write my story, for I wish to give hope and encouragement to someone out there, be it a migrant child or just someone who feels unwanted, unloved …

Photograph credits

Except for those noted below, photographs used on the cover and within this book are, and remain, the property of the author and/or her family.

Page 31: Two women smoking opium, original source unknown. https://kknews.cc/history/4o63a5q.html. Accessed 15 Aug 2022.

Page 41: A column of smoke from burning rubber rises over the trees on a Malayan rubber plantation during the British retreat to Singapore. December 1941. Photographer: Fred Palmer (Hon Lt). Photograph KF 97 from the collections of the Imperial War Museums. https://commons.wikimedia.org/wiki/File:Malayan_rubber_plantation_burning.jpg. Accessed 14 Aug 2022.

Page 57: Feet of a Chinese woman showing the effect of footbinding. Photograph 19 Wellcome Collection. Public Domain Mark 1.0 https://wellcomecollection.org/works/zhvjpvnk/images?id=f34gdwen. Accessed 21 Aug 2022.

Page 64: North Bridge Road, Singapore, 1941-1945, Photographer: Mr Colin Keon-Cohen. Creative Commons Attribution 4.0 International licence. Museums Victoria Collections https://collections.museumsvictoria.com.au/items/1797287. Accessed 5 September 2022.

Page 108: Victoria Institute Girls of 1958, Lower Sixth & Upper Sixth. The V.I. Image Gallery. http://www.viweb.school/viig_Girls1958.htm. Accessed 6 November 2022.

Page 114: Linda Lin Dai's film still from Golden Lotus (1957) by Cathay-Keris Films Pte Ltd. http://www.info.gov.hk/gia/general/200907/15/P200907150195.htm, Public Domain, https://commons.wikimedia.org/w/index.php?curid=94170595. Accessed 4 Sep 2022.

Page 186: Terracotta Army Pit 1 in Xi'an, China. Photographer: Maros Mraz. Multi-license with GFDL and Creative Commons CC-BY-SA-2.5 and older versions. https://en.wikipedia.org/wiki/File:Terracotta_Army_Pit_1_-_2.jpg. Accessed 19 Sep 2022.

Page 201: Statue of Sun Yat-Sen as a schoolboy in front of the Sun Yat-Sen Museum, Kom Tong Hall in Hong Kong. Author:

Cheanguehuae, CC BY-SA 3.0 <https://creativecommons.org/licenses/by-sa/3.0>, via Wikimedia Commons. https://commons.wikimedia.org/wiki/File:HK_Mid-levels_Kom_Tong_Hall_Sun_Yat-sen_Museum_01_Statue.JPG. Accessed 6 November 2022.

Page 212: "Flemington, Melbourne" by Samuel Charles Brees, c. 1856, Courtesy of the State Library Victoria. https://victoriancollections.net.au/stories/many-roads-stories-of-the-chinese-on-the-goldfields/walking-to-the-diggings. Accessed 16 Sep 2022.

Page 215: Male Gang Gang parrot, author JJ Harrison, https://www.jjharrison.com.au/. Licensed under the Creative Commons Attribution-Share Alike 3.0 Unported license. Accessed 16 Sep 2022.

Page 226: View of the Parramatta River from Rivendell School, Concord West. © State of New South Wales (Department of Education), 2021. Creative Commons Attribution 4.0 International licence. https://rivendell-s.schools.nsw.gov.au/. Accessed 16 Sep 2022.

Back cover: The Bund Shanghai, China, 1928. Good Free Photos via: <a href="https://www.goodfreephotos.com/">Good Free Photos</a>. Accessed 6 Aug 2022.

www.ingramcontent.com/pod-product-compliance
Lightning Source LLC
Chambersburg PA
CBHW050308010526
44107CB00055B/2154